Praise for *Splitting Up Together*

"An easy to understand practical how-to guide on amicably divorcing. A must read for anyone in the process of or thinking about splitting up"

"This book goes to show that divorce doesn't have to become ugly and complicated. There is a clear simple, process that can be followed to avoid ending up in court fighting"

"A ripper of a book that deserves a place in bookstores everywhere"

"Many people out there will benefit hugely from such straightforward and clear writing"

"A very practical, helpful useful book that fills a gap in the marketplace"

"I found it to be thought provoking; answering questions that I didn't even know I had. It made me consider my relationship in a different light. I'd recommend this book to anyone who is thinking about divorce or who is going through one"

Splitting Up Together

The How-to Handbook for an **AMICABLE** Divorce

Siobhan E Mullins

Published by Separate Together Pty Ltd 2019

Copyright © 2019 by Siobhan E. Mullins

Separate Together Pty Ltd is an incorporated legal practice in the Australian Capital Territory, trading as Separate Together.

All rights reserved. No part of this publication may be reproduced, stored in a retrieval system, or transmitted in any form or by any means, electronic, mechanical, photocopying, recording or otherwise, without prior written permission from both the copyright owner and publisher.

Disclaimer: This publication is intended to be an information source only. It is sold on the basis of the terms and understanding that the publisher, author and editors are not responsible for any outcomes as a result of actions taken in purported reliance on any part of the publication, nor any error in, or omission from this publication. The publisher, author and editors expressly disclaim all or any liability (including liability for negligence) and responsibility to any reader for the consequences, financial or otherwise, of anything done or omitted to be done by any person in purported reliance on the material contained in this publication.

The commentary contained within this book on legislation, case law, and any precedent contained within this book does not constitute legal advice or legal services and should not be relied on for that purpose or any related purpose. Any information and content in this book is general in nature only, and does not take into account the objectives and needs of any particular person. Any reader should consult and take advice from a competent and suitably qualified professional regarding their own particular situation.

National Library of Australia Cataloguing-in-Publication details:
Author: Mullins, Siobhan Elizabeth Mary
Title: Splitting Up Together: The How-to Handbook for an AMICABLE Divorce/Siobhan Mullins
Subjects: Law, self-help & personal development, separation, divorce
Book cover design and formatting service SelfPublishingLab.com

First edition 2019
ISBN 978-0-9876326-0-9 (pbk)
ISBN 978-0-9876326-1-6 (e-bk)

Currency
The author and publisher intend that the law and commentary is current at 31 December 2018.

Ready to separate?

To get advice or help preparing your separation agreement paperwork, visit:

separatetogether.com.au

or call

(02) 6100 3629

Dedicated to:
My biggest supporter, my brother,
Liam Mullins, for everything.
My grandfather, whose eyes lit up when we talked about my business and whose 'why-not' attitude continues to encourage me.

Contents

Foreword	xi
Acknowledgements	xv
Introduction	xvii
1 Making the Decision to Separate	1
2 Acceptance	25
3 Momentum	35
4 Interests	51
5 Consider your Backup Plan	57
6 Advice	69
7 Brainstorm	89
8 LEADR to Yes	93
9 Endorse Your Agreement	103
• The benefits	
• Parenting agreements	
• Financial agreements	
• Child support	
• Maintenance	
• Divorce	
10 Putting It All into Practice	129

Download Your Free Kick-Starter Separation Pack	141
About the Author	143
Bibliography	145

Foreword

When Siobhan told me that she was writing a book for people facing separation and the prospect of litigation to resolve issues arising from it, I was intrigued. When I received the initial draft 100 page manuscript, and finished reading it, I was confident that the book would provide a much needed plain English guide to assist people get through their separation and finalise the legal aspects of the termination of their relationship.

I have practised in family law, equity/trusts and guardianship and protected estates since 1976, the year in which the Family Law Act (Cth) 1975 came into force. The Act first made provision for counselling services and conciliation as means to resolve family law disputes without the need to resort to a contested hearing by the Courts. The Courts have increasingly encouraged parties to disputes to resolve them by alternative dispute resolution, which now includes mediation in addition to the original means of counselling and conciliation. In circumstances where Australia's family law system and the legislation applying to it are being reviewed, this book is a timely reminder about the need to emphasise dispute resolution as an alternative to contested court proceedings.

Siobhan's goal to empower readers by educating them about the need to know information about the legal system is readily fulfilled by the contents of this book. It provides necessary information for someone who is contemplating separation or who has separated, with appropriate encouragement to readers to seek from professionals further specific advice and strategy relevant to them, whether that advice be legal, psychological or financial.

This book balances legal information with practical guidance about separation—the consequences, the logistics and the practical emotional and financial aspects of separation.

Noteworthy is the breakdown of seemingly complex legal concepts into easy to understand plain English, thereby allowing readers to follow the book and avoid feeling overwhelmed.

Siobhan has clearly written this book with the reader in mind. The book's structure builds on the foundational layers of information established as one reads through the book and with Siobhan's use of language and turn of phrase, you could say it's almost like having a conversation with Siobhan in person.

In writing this book, Siobhan has clearly drawn on her experience as a lawyer and from her successful business, Separate Together, applying her knowledge of the law, her understanding of the problems people face even before separating and her appreciation of their need for assistance at a difficult time of their lives. Every effort is made to inform the reader and give them confidence in their ability to take control of their relationship and to identify and resolve the issues surrounding its termination.

Included throughout is some commentary from clients and case studies that apply the point that is being made to effectively convey the message to the reader.

Siobhan raises the importance of getting a reality check on one's expectations from qualified professionals as part of the process. This is important because inadequate or misleading advice can contribute to people proceeding to litigation with the associated delays, cost and anxiety, which could have been avoided by well-informed decision making.

Splitting Up Together is a worthwhile read for anyone who wants to know more about the legal separation process, one's options when it comes to remaining together or separating, what the law says in general terms about appropriate family law outcomes and ways to avoid contested litigation.

This handbook will answer more questions than it raises and is the starting place for someone who is contemplating separating or who is anywhere along the divorce journey.

Julian Millar
Barrister
4th Floor Wentworth Chambers
Sydney

Acknowledgements

My brother, Liam, has been my biggest cheerleader and supporter. I don't have enough words to thank Liam for all he has done for me.

Thank you to my mum and dad, who've instilled in me my work ethic and shown me how one can make a career out of a passion for helping people. I wouldn't be where I am today without either of them.

Thank you to my brother, Sean, for his never-ending encouragement and patience. Thank you to my brother, Patrick, and my sister-in-law, Kate, for all the laughs and their support in this journey.

Thank you to Julian Millar, whose support, intellect, dedication and passion for family law I am in awe of. Thank you to Norm Green, for his business insight, words of wisdom and support.

Thank you to the KPI community—in particular Brigid for her contribution—for making this book all the more human and relatable.

Thank you to my best friends, and to those family lawyers I also call friends, who have supported me in what I set out to do.

Lastly, thank you to my clients from whom I've learnt so much.

Introduction

Who this book is for

Are you thinking of separating, or are you recently separated? Are you feeling overwhelmed, like you don't have control? Don't know what to do next?

Then this book is for you.

Splitting Up Together isn't a touchy-feely emotional book. It is a book for those who want to learn how the legal separation process works, the steps that are involved and the way separate to minimise fees, conflict and reduce lawyer involvement, all the while avoiding court. Splitting Up Together is for those who aspire to have an amicable separation and want a roadmap of the separation journey ahead.

There are plenty of wishy-washy self-help and legalese books on breakups, but until now there has been no plain-English, easy-to-understand handbook on the practical stuff to do and think about before and after separation.

How this book will help you

Couples who end up in court are there because they've been unable to reach an agreement together about the split of their finances, parenting, child support or maintenance, and they need a judge to make a decision for them. The way to avoid court, lawyers and expensive legal fees is to reach an agreement with your partner, but this can be hard.

Knowing where to begin even before you've separated, and understanding the legal process and what your next steps should be to reach an agreement can be confusing and daunting. I believe that only with the right information and attitude can you and your partner commit to having an amicable separation. By providing the right information, this book will up skill, and educate you to reach a separation agreement. After reading it, you will feel empowered and in control of your separation so that when or if the decision to separate is made you'll know exactly what to do.

You'll notice that throughout this book I refer to your 'partner', not your 'ex', and not 'the bastard' or 'the witch'. Now you might have a new partner, boyfriend or girlfriend, but the reason I refer to your ex as your 'partner' is because you both need to remain and work as a team in order to finalise your separation quickly.

INTRODUCTION

You and your partner don't have to be amicable to finalise your separation quickly and easily. All you need to do is use my AMICABLE method, which is a process methodology stepping out the typical steps that you'll go through as part of your separation journey.

AMICABLE is an acronym that stands for:

- *Acceptance:* Accepting that the relationship is over.
- *Momentum*: The practical things you need to do in order to reach an agreement with your partner.
- *Interests*: Identify interests; the needs, goals and priorities that will help you and your partner reach a final agreement.
- *Consideration*: Consider your backup plan if you and your partner don't reach a final agreement.
- *Advice*: Counsel from a professional to give you a reality check about your expectations.
- *Brainstorming*: Brainstorm potential agreement outcomes with your partner that, with some improvement, could lead to a final agreement outcome that satisfies your and your partner's interests.
- *LEADR to yes*: A structured framework for your agreement discussion that stands for listen, express, acknowledge, discuss, repeat.
- *Endorse*: Make your agreement official.

After reading *Splitting Up Together* you will be armed with the following knowledge:

- What to consider when separating
- Definition of the term 'legally separate'
- Changes to expect after separation
- Common mistakes people make when separating and how to avoid them
- Whether you need to see a lawyer, and the tasks you can complete yourself that don't require a lawyer
- What the law says in general terms about divorce, child support, maintenance, financial splits and parenting after separation
- Advice you should consider getting from different professionals and why
- The different ways you can make your separation agreements official
- How, by following my AMICABLE method, you can reach a separation agreement

My story

Growing up, I wanted to be a teacher—and I'd be lying if I said it wasn't in part because I liked kids and the idea of regular holidays. Basically, I saw (and still see) education as a way of helping and empowering people through knowledge.

With a keen interest in wanting to help people, I initially began studying social work at university, before then transferring and finishing with a degree in social science and following this up with a law degree.

My first legal job was working as a paralegal at a small family law firm, before becoming a lawyer. Aside from a brief three-month stint in the public service, I've worked exclusively in family law since 2011.

It's been the crossover between my passion for wanting to help people through education and me having always been a little bit different to my peers (which my mum calls unique) that led to me establish my family law firm, Separate Together.

Separate Together is different from traditional family law firms in its area of speciality—being to help separating individuals and couples prepare the paperwork to make their separation agreements official. Separate Together is an online firm that does not go to Court, instead focusing on educating people about how to make their separation agreements official. The firm's integration of technology facilitates people preparing their own draft paperwork at affordable fixed prices, where lawyer involvement is optional.

Family law is typically perceived as doom and gloom but I'm fortunate to work in a space where I see positive divorce and separation stories. The individuals and couples who I work with inspire me daily with their attitude and commitment to set aside their differences to prioritise their health, their emotional and financial well being and their children in order to successfully separate, but together.

Why I wrote this book

Even before making the decision to separate, people often face the problem of not knowing where to start, they perceive the separation process to be too hard and too complicated and that they have to use a lawyer—which they want to avoid because of expensive legal fees and conflict, and their deep fear that they'll end up in court.

I wrote this book because I wanted to try and alleviate people feeling too overwhelmed, stressed and not in control. I believe:

- You deserve a simple, easy to understand how-to roadmap about the legal separation process.
- You deserve an unbiased, no nonsense handbook that focuses on the practicalities of separation,

your options when it comes to staying together or separating, how you can reach an agreement, your options when it comes to make that agreement official and how you can reduce lawyer involvement.
- You can benefit from me sharing the knowledge that I have about the law, my observations as a divorce lawyer and about people's experience

I want to empower people who are going through or considering separation through education with the right information to then enable them to make informed decisions. Doing so can help shape people's attitudes and approach to their own separation, helping them to commit to an amicable separation.

Getting the most out of this book

Splitting Up Together is the culmination of my experience as a divorce lawyer working with family law clients representing them at court, mediation, negotiating and collaborating on their behalf, drafting legal documents and providing legal advice. This book is the result of what I know about the law, what I've learnt and my interactions and observations of people as a divorce lawyer over the years.

If you're at the point of trying to make a decision about whether to separate or not, you need only read chapter 1. The point of chapter 1 is to give you some practical things to consider as part of your decision process, your options when it comes to staying together or not, and to provide a high level overview about the legal separation process—what the law says in general terms, your options to reach an agreement together and how to make it official.

When you feel ready, then I encourage you to read the whole book, which goes into more detail about the legal separation process.

Take your time to familiarise yourself with the book from start to finish. Don't over think or get ahead of yourself. I intend for this book to be a practical resource for you to go back to, write notes and do the exercises. It's completely up to you whether you do them as you go through the book or whether you wait until you're ready or have read the entire book.

By the end, you'll see how everything pulls together and how the exercises will help you. By committing to having an amicable separation, and by doing the practical exercises, the AMICABLE method can work for you, just as it has for many others.

I have used legal terms that are referred to in the legislation, namely the *Family Law Act 1975*. I've unpacked what the legal terms mean where appropriate, but have not referenced specific sections of the law. I have used quotation marks with these words and phrases but have not added a reference.

I have sought to achieve a balance between appropriate referencing and readability by referring to sources within the text. Full details of the sources referred to are provided in the Bibliography.

Chapter 1
Making the Decision to Separate

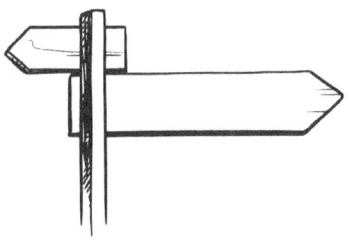

If you've picked up this book, you might be considering separation, or you and your partner have already separated, whether one or both of you have made that decision.

You needn't read the entirety of this book to get a complete understanding about the immediate need-to-know information because in this chapter I will cover several important areas. You'll therefore have a high level understanding about each of these areas, enough to feel reassured about the separation process and the potential journey ahead. I'll go into more detail about each of these areas in the later chapters so that you have a more complete understanding:

- Making the decision to separate
- Your options, whether separating or staying together
- The meaning of the term 'legally separate'
- Who to tell if you separate
- Changes to expect after you separate
- How and where to get advice
- The legal separation process explained

You can see that you'll probably learn more from this chapter alone about the legal separation process and the practical things you want to think about when separating than you would if you were to meet with a divorce lawyer and pay them several hundred dollars. Consider your money in buying this book well spent!

Making the decision to separate

Making the decision to separate requires some reflection on your part. The first thing to work out is whether you're

CHAPTER 1: MAKING THE DECISION TO SEPARATE

in the right headspace to be making any life-changing decisions right now.

The decision to separate can be an easy one for some people, particularly if there are complex issues like violence, lies, infidelity or other deep-seated problems. But even without these sorts of issues, it can be an extremely hard decision to make, let alone have imposed on you. It can be particularly difficult if you have children because you probably want what is best for them, and working out what that means may not be easy.

Life events, and sometimes life in general, can lead us to question our relationships with significant others, friends, family and work colleagues. The first exercise I want you to do is to simply sit for a moment and reflect. Then read through this list and decide whether you or your partner have experienced any of these events in the last eighteen months that could be affecting your headspace:

- Miscarriage
- Pregnancy and/or birth
- Physical or emotional cheating
- Physical violence/verbal abuse
- Career change (change of job, termination)
- Death of a family member or friend
- Gambling/addiction issues

- Criminal offence/victim of crime
- Moved interstate or overseas
- Car accident
- Mental-illness diagnosis/suspicion of you/your partner (including depression)
- Diagnosis of a mental illness or depression-like symptoms

It could be a combination of one or more of the above, or none. You and your partner could simply have a lot going on at the moment in your life, whether it's work, the kids, sick parents, or you just aren't getting on.

Do you need a break to have time to think about your relationship? If yes, what are you going to do about it? It is important to tap into the reasons behind the question mark over your relationship.

> *I ended up speaking with a counsellor, who really helped me to understand what was going on. My ex and I got together when we were in our early twenties; we had two boys together, and, in hindsight, got married for the wrong reasons. As we got older, we grew up. We both changed and came to realise that we wanted different things in life.*

CHAPTER 1: MAKING THE DECISION TO SEPARATE

The next part of this exercise involves getting out your phone and going into the notes app, or grabbing a pen and paper. Write down the top five things that keep you awake at night. Which of these top five things do you believe are caused—directly or indirectly—by your partner? Write them down. Are any of them deal-breakers? Is there anything that could be fixed?

Now put your notes to one side and have a think about your relationship. The point of this next exercise is to help you reflect on whether the relationship is going through a rough patch that you could possibly work through together, or if separating is the right decision for you.

It can take weeks, months or even years to make the decision to separate, and it can represent a massive change in your life, so be patient. I've worked with people who have come to see me for initial advice well before they making the final decision to separate.

Here are a few suggestions that might help you in your soul-searching when it comes to making that decision:

- Consider your values and attitudes about family, career, money, parenting, children. What are your partner's values and attitude towards these things? Are your values and attitudes consistent with one

another or different? Do any differences need to be worked through? Can they be worked through?
- Do you and your partner share any common goals? What are they?
- Identify your physical, intellectual, emotional and psychological needs (for example, physical intimacy, intellectual stimulation, emotional support, affection).
- Which of those needs does your partner currently satisfy?
- Which of those needs do you want or need your partner to satisfy?
- Identify your partner's physical, intellectual, emotional and psychological needs.
- Which of your partner's needs do you think you satisfy?
- What can you see your life looking like five years from now if you separate from your partner?
- What can you see your life looking like five years from now if you are still together?

Writing down your answers to the above questions may help with your reflection and consideration of the relationship.

CHAPTER 1: MAKING THE DECISION TO SEPARATE

Interesting facts

- In a 2011 survey by Relationships Australia, respondents cited four main reasons for their relationship ending: being financial stress, communication difficulties, different expectations and values, and a lack of trust.
  According to this survey, fewer people are getting married these days and more people are living together before they marry, if at all. Perhaps unsurprisingly, the survey identified that more people are having children together and not marrying.

- The Australian Bureau of Statistics (2016) identifies that in 2016, the median age of men and women marrying for the first time was 31.9 years and 29.9 years respectively. The 2016 data identifies the median length of a marriage from the date of the marriage to separation was 8.4 years and that the median age of divorce for males and females in 2016 was 45.5 and 42.9 years respectively.

- A key finding in relation to marriage breakdown is that women are twice as likely to initiate separation than their male counterparts (Hewitt 2008, p. 25).

Your options, whether separating or staying together

You can choose to explore separating or staying together in several different ways before actually making the decision:

- Do it yourself: You and your partner can try communicating with one another, reading the self-help books, having date nights, or going on romantic trips or couples' retreats with professionals to see if these things improve your relationship.
- Individual counselling: You can have one-on-one sessions with a counsellor, psychologist or psychiatrist to work on yourself, any perceived deal-breakers, the relationship; or examine your decision about whether to separate or stay together.
- Couples counselling: You can both go to counselling to work on the relationship, discuss your value alignment, reconcile, or get help working through the process of separating together.
- Workshops: You can participate in a communication course or workshop with or without your partner to see what affect, if any, it has on your relationship and your decision to separate or stay together.

As much as you both may try, however, the deep soul-searching, weekends away and date nights may still be a flop. There might be nothing left in the relationship tank; perhaps it has holes that just can't be mended, and no matter how much you keep refilling it, it continues to leak.

CHAPTER 1: MAKING THE DECISION TO SEPARATE

The pit in your stomach when you think about separating—the impact on your kids, friends, extended family and your partner, and your financial position—is understandable. Separation is scary. But you will get through this, because I will help you when or if you make the decision to separate.

The meaning of the term 'legally separate'

The legal definition of separation involves any couple in a romantic relationship (being two people, whether the same or different sex) that has been 'brought to an end by the action or conduct of a person to the relationship'. Basically, one of you has put an end to you being a romantically involved couple. It's important to note that you can be separated while still living together under the same roof.

You or your partner might decide that you'll continue living under the same roof until you sort out how you'll split your finances or arrange for your children's care. There can be pros and cons to moving out or staying in the same house together (which I cover in a later chapter).

> *My ex and I decided that we'd keep living together under the same roof after we separated until we worked out the kids' custody and how we were going to split our assets. It was good on the one hand because it meant that the kids still had stability in seeing us both every day, and we kept our finances the same as before so we didn't have to pay for two households immediately. It was a bit uncomfortable at times having to be around one another, but we made it a priority to work together and put on a brave face for the kids.*

Who to tell if you separate

Aside from telling your partner that you want to separate, you may want to consider the following:

- You're not required to sign or lodge any documents with the court to let them know that you've separated.
- If you receive Centrelink entitlements (for example, family tax benefit, family assistance, childcare subsidy, schoolkids bonus, youth allowance, AusStudy), you are obligated to tell Centrelink about the change in circumstances of your relationship. If you have kids,

Centrelink may automatically issue a formal child-support assessment.
- If either you or your partner is on a visa in Australia, you are required to tell the Department of Home Affairs about the change in your relationship status.
- It may be in your interests to let your accountant, financial advisor/planner and bank know that you have separated.
- You may want to consider letting your GP, counsellor, psychiatrist or psychologist know so they can support you appropriately.
- You may want or need to tell your child's daycare, babysitter or school so your kids can be appropriately supported in that environment, too.

Changes to expect after you separate

After the decision to separate has been made, you might experience immediate day-to-day physical changes:

- Changes to your living situation: You might move out of the home you share with your partner, your partner might move out, or one of you may begin sleeping in separate bedrooms or in different parts of the house if you haven't already.

- Changes to your career/work hours: You may need to increase your work hours to make ends meet financially, or reduce your work hours in order to care for your kids.
- Changes to your finances: You may decide to separate your finances, which could increase or decrease your living or household expenses.
- Changes in the time you spend time with your kids: You and your partner may need to decide whether you will spend time with the children one on one separately and apart from the other parent, or whether the children will live primarily with one of you and spend time with the other parent.

The immediate intangible things that you may experience:

- Feeling that an emotional weight has been lifted
- A sense of freedom when you and your partner speak or interact with each other
- Fights, arguments, silent treatment, depression or tears
- Relief, a sense of freedom and/or happiness
- Feelings of dread, regret, depression, anger or sadness

Thinking longer term, separation will inevitably affect both of your lives. I often encourage my clients to look beyond the next twelve months and think longer term; specifically, how life is inevitably going to change. Having some foresight and understanding about life ahead means that you can 'try on' separation—see what it might look like—before you commit to it.

There are several things that you need to be aware of:

- Two households requiring financial support: Your pie (your joint assets and debts, including superannuation in joint names and separate names combined) may not stretch to financially supporting two households at the standard of living you're used to.
- Financial care of children: Your ability to financially provide for your children may be limited. You might not be able to afford the same opportunities you would have if you'd stayed together, for example, private-school fees, extracurricular activities, overseas holidays and medical expenses.
- Maintenance: Depending on your financial circumstances, you might be entitled to receive maintenance from your partner, or required to pay maintenance to your partner.

- Living arrangements: There will likely be changes to your children's living arrangements. This could see you spending more or less time with your children than you currently do. You and your partner may decide to see your children on birthdays and other milestones, graduations, Christmases, weddings and the like separately. You might go weeks at a time not seeing your kids because they are with your partner.
- Care of sick children: Depending on the children's ages and your support network—people who can care for them when sick or during the school holidays—you may have to take unpaid leave from work, purchase additional leave, or use up your annual, long-service or sick leave entitlements to care for them.
- Financial support: You may need to re-enter the workforce or increase your work hours to support yourself financially. You may also need to undertake further study or gain qualifications, which could take time.

How and where to get advice

Getting advice and information from a professional early on, before you separate, is a good idea because you can get perspective and a reality check about what your life could look like after separation. Professionals you could consult include a:

- Mortgage broker, who could talk to you about your borrowing capacity, and your ability to service a loan when it comes to buying or keeping a property
- 'Numbers person' (financial planner, advisor or accountant), who could talk to you about managing money, your budget, expenditure, re-establishing yourself financially after separation, funding your children's expenses, and preparation for retirement
- Child psychologist, who could talk to you about how to meet your children's needs now and going forward if you do separate
- Family lawyer, who could talk to you about what would be an appropriate outcome for you in relation to a financial split, parenting, child support, maintenance and divorce

The legal separation process

It can be difficult knowing where to start and what to do once the decision to separate has been made. But your end goal is to reach an agreement with your partner and consider making it official. Couples that end up in court are there because, for whatever reason, they've been unable to reach an agreement together, and one of them has asked the court for a judge to make a decision for them.

Parenting matters: Let's say you and your partner have kids together and you can't reach an agreement about their care arrangements. You would normally be required to attend mediation first to try and reach an agreement before either of you can ask the court for a judge to make a decision.

If you go to mediation and can't agree, or mediation isn't appropriate for whatever reason, or you or your partner refuse to participate, then you can ask the court for a judge to make a decision for you without going through mediation, which they will do in the form of a parenting court order (more about this in a later chapter).

In very broad general terms, to get the court involved you both have to prepare paperwork that sets out what you want as a final parenting outcome, and gives evidence justifying your desired outcome. This paperwork is submitted to the court, and you and your partner then have to attend a court hearing, where a judge may make court orders that are intended to help steer you in the direction of a decision about your children's care arrangements.

CHAPTER 1: MAKING THE DECISION TO SEPARATE

Often the court will require you, your partner and your children (and potentially any other significant person in your children's lives) to meet for an interview with a child expert (a court-appointed family consultant). The child expert will provide a written report with recommendations regarding your children's care.

Many parents use this report to reach an agreement together without having to go to trial and have a judge make a decision for them. For those parents who are unable to agree, the judge will consider the expert's report, together with evidence from each parent, and make a decision that leads to a parenting court order.

Financial matters: Let's say you and your partner can't agree about the split of your finances. Before asking the court to make a decision for you, you have to exchange your financial documents (this is covered in chapter 3).

Before starting the court proceedings, 'all genuine efforts to resolve the matter [must] have failed'.

Similar to parenting disagreements, in order to get the court involved, you and your partner have to prepare paperwork that sets out what you want as a financial split, and provides evidence justifying your outcome. This paperwork is submitted to the court.

You and your partner then have to attend a court hearing date, where a judge makes orders intended to steer you in the direction of a decision being made about an appropriate financial split.

The court may order that you and your partner attend a financial mediation. Where this financial mediation is to occur before a registrar (being a lawyer of the court), it is called a conciliation conference.

According to the Federal Circuit Court's 2017–18 Annual Report, 36 percent of the registrar-facilitated conciliation conferences settled—meaning 36 percent of those separating couples who had initially asked for a judge to make a decision for them—managed to reach an agreement about their financial split at their conference.

If you don't reach an agreement, usually you have to return before a judge who'll make orders listing your matter for trial in twelve-plus months' time.

Different types of agreements

Matters that generally need to be worked out after you and your partner separate may include:

- If you have children together, an agreement about your children's care arrangements and all

things relating to them, including child support (periodic and non-periodic expenses, for example, extracurricular activities, medical and dental)
- The split of the pie: assets, debts and superannuation (formally called your 'property settlement')
- Maintenance: ongoing financial support
- Applying for divorce

The AMICABLE method

You don't have to be that couple that can't reach an agreement. Do you remember Gwyneth Paltrow and Chris Martin deciding that they would 'consciously uncouple'? A lot of us divorce lawyers cringed at this term, but the principle is a good one. What if you could separate but still be able to talk to your partner? Well, you can.

Without the mung beans and kale, I have developed the AMICABLE method. This method identifies the steps that will help you reach an agreement with your partner after separation. Sounds good, right? Let's get to it.

As explained in detail in chapter 1, AMICABLE is an acronym that stands for acceptance, momentum, interests, consideration, advice, brainstorming, LEADR-to-yes, and endorse.

Options for reaching an agreement

You and your partner don't have to go to court. You can choose to reach an agreement in a variety of ways:

- Get together and talk: Follow my AMICABLE method and have kitchen-table negotiations. Simply get together, talk and reach an agreement without involving a third person
- Mediation: Participate in mediation through a mediation service or a third person (for example, a trusted friend, family member or professional mediator).
- Consult a professional: Speak with a professional to help you agree. You could speak with your trusted accountant, financial advisor/planner about finances. You could speak with a child psychologist or counsellor about your children's care arrangements.
- Solicitor-aided mediation: This is where you both have your own lawyer and participate in mediation.
- Lawyer letter-writing negotiation: Engage a lawyer to write and respond to your partner on your behalf, putting forward different agreement proposals.
- Parenting agreement: You can participate in child-inclusive mediation, which assesses and incorporates children's views as part of the mediation.

Another option is collaborative family law. Collaborative family law is where you and your partner each have a lawyer and everyone works together as one team to achieve an agreement outcome that is consistent with your interests. It is a process whereby you negotiate on interests (needs, goals, priorities) rather than a traditional positional bargaining approach.

You both sign a legally binding contract saying that you won't go to court or use threats of going to court. If you go through the collaborative-family-law process and don't reach an agreement, you cannot use your lawyers in court proceedings. (There is the obvious financial incentive of sticking with the collaboration so you don't waste money having to engage new lawyers).

Making the agreement official

I believe that making your agreement official is probably the easiest part in a separation because you've already done the hard work in reaching an agreement together. There are different ways you can make your agreement official:

- Parenting separation agreement: You can make the agreement official in a parenting plan or parenting consent orders.

- Financial separation agreement: You can make the agreement official in a binding financial agreement or financial consent order. If you're wondering about statutory declarations, deeds and napkin agreements, they don't cut it. They're not legally recognised and they're not binding. Why? Because the law simply doesn't recognise agreements in that way. The court doesn't get to see the agreement, and the people signing up to the deal aren't required to have independent legal advice.
- Child support: You might choose to leave this as assessed by the child-support agency, include in a parenting plan or make it official in a limited child-support agreement or a binding child-support agreement.
- Maintenance agreement: Whether there will be ongoing financial support, or no ongoing financial support, you can make the agreement official in a binding financial agreement.

I go into more detail about these agreements in chapter 9.

Applying for divorce

To apply to the court for a divorce order, you and your partner have to be separated for more than twelve months.

There is some additional paperwork to do if you've been living separated under one roof in the twelve months leading up to applying for divorce, or, if you've been married for less than two years, there are additional steps you have to do first before you can apply.

Time limits

There are important time limits to consider:

- De facto couples have two years from the date of their separation to make their financial separation agreement official.
- Married couples have twelve months from the date of their divorce to make their financial separation agreements official.
- There are no time limits when it comes to parenting and child-support matters.

Chapter 2

Acceptance

Acceptance that the relationship is over is the first step to being able to progress the separation effectively. In this chapter I will give insight into the stages of grief you and your partner will go through in coming to terms with your separation, from which you'll gain understanding about one another's behaviours. I'll also show you how you're going to look after yourself through the separation process and explain to you why this is important. Finally, I'll discuss the mistakes that people commonly make and how you're going to avoid them.

Stages of grief

In their book, *On Grief and Grieving*, Elisabeth Kubler-Ross and David Kessler (2005) discuss the five stages of grief as they apply to death. These principles also apply to relationship breakdown. The first stage is denial, followed up anger, bargaining, depression and, finally, acceptance.

From my experience in working with separating couples, I know that when someone pushes themselves or their partner along in the grief process before they are both ready it creates resistance, distrust and conflict, and disengagement by the person who is still grieving the relationship.

> *Although the writing had been on the wall for some time that my ex-wife and I were heading for a divorce, when she finally told me that she wanted a divorce, I was really surprised. I remember being angry, pissed off and pretty depressed initially. She seemed fine with it all, which hurt. It took me a while, but I managed to work through what I was*

CHAPTER 2: ACCEPTANCE

feeling and she was patient with me. In hindsight, I think if she'd pushed me to hurry up before I was ready, then we wouldn't have the relationship that we have today. We're still on good talking terms and have family dinners every so often with the kids.

It's important that you understand the grief process so you can develop insight into your partner's behaviour and actions, and your own, to avoid making the mistake of rushing the grieving process.

So, has the writing been on the wall for some time that a separation is on the cards? Or are you or your partner in utter shock or surprise?

My good friend, Brigid, says that when she told her ex-partner she wanted to separate he was shocked to learn that anything was wrong with their relationship. Brigid told me that her ex had missed all the signs that she was ready to separate. She tried the counselling, the dinners and the holidays. 'In hindsight,' Brigid told me, 'I think I stayed in the denial phase for a good six months before actually committing to the decision to separate and then telling my ex.' There is the saying, women grieve before they leave (source unknown).

This is unsurprising and fairly common. You may be thinking about separating for months or years before you commit to it and say it aloud to your partner. You may then have already quietly started the grieving process. In Brigid's case, she was already at the acceptance phase or at the end of the grief cycle.

Knowing where your partner is at in the grief cycle is helpful in building empathy and moving them towards better decisions. A word of caution: the grief process isn't always linear; sometimes people can remain at different points for a long time, or even cycle backwards in the grief process.

Have you both decided to separate? A mutual decision would suggest that you have both started the grieving process.

Is your partner in their own world? Sometimes the hardest part of a separation can be working with a partner who is divorced from reality (excuse the pun). It can be hard to know where they are emotionally in the grieving process, and difficult to respond appropriately because they appear to be out of touch with reality, having little insight into or understanding of their actions. They may not appreciate the effect of their actions on you and the family unit.

So, what do you do? It's a hard one, because you can't control them and you're unlikely to be able to reason with them. You'll likely end up 'managing' them. This could be described as playing a strategic game of chess while taking care not to annoy them.

CHAPTER 2: ACCEPTANCE

Look after yourself

The reality is that no one will look after you but you. Harsh, but true. At times in this process you will want to look after your partner, and sometimes you will want your partner to look after you, but this is your new single reality: you do you.

Separation is already hard enough, and taking steps to progress it will inevitably take its toll emotionally, mentally, spiritually and physically. If you don't prioritise taking care of yourself, then the path ahead will be that much harder. Your ability to be an effective parent, friend, business owner, work colleague or employee is likely to be negatively affected.

You're going to begin taking care of yourself by creating a happy-stuff list. Get your mobile phone and go into the notes app, or grab a pen and paper. Write down those things that make you happy. It might be catching up with friends for a drink, playing sport, going to the gym, seeing a movie, reading a book or getting a massage—whatever it is, write it down.

Get moving. If you don't have a physical activity on your list, write one down, even if it's just going for a fifteen-minute walk every day.

There are four major chemicals in the brain that can influence happiness: dopamine, oxytocin, serotonin and endorphins. Endorphins are the chemicals that are released after physical exercise. Aside from the physical benefits of moving, psychologically there are benefits, too.

Commit to doing more of the happy stuff by diarising at least one activity in your happy-stuff list that you will do every second day (three to four times per week).

The next thing you're going to do is to tell a minimum of three people about the happy-stuff and your commitment to do at least one happy-stuff activity every second day, minimum. Ask them to check in with you weekly to see if you've done it.

Go on. Do it now. I'll wait.

Getting other people to hold you accountable will help you to prioritise doing the happy-stuff, thereby prioritising your happiness.

The other thing you're going to do is surround yourself with a supportive network; that can be your friends, family, GP, counsellor or lawyer. It's up to you when you tell the right people at the right time about the separation, even if you do it gradually over a period of time.

Common mistakes

There are several common mistakes that people make when separating, but they can be avoided.

CHAPTER 2: ACCEPTANCE

Mistake #1: Rushing the separation or divorce: I've explained the logic behind you and your partner needing to accept that the relationship is ending first before embarking on the legal separation process. This will help with the grief cycle and put you in the right headspace to be more objective. Take your time to breathe. You both need to be able to moderate the level of emotion that you're experiencing before moving forward.

Mistake #2: Not seeing yourself as a team: You were partners in a relationship and now you have to be partners in a new type of relationship—the separated kind. In order to get through the separation, you'll need to work together as a team. You're on the same side. To invoke the feeling of teamwork, use positive affirmative language such as 'we' and 'our', for example, 'How are we going to move forward?' or 'What things do we need to do in order to sort this?' This language helps embody the feeling of control and ownership of the process.

Mistake #3: Making assumptions: If you feel insecure or vulnerable, or you're in an unstable, uncertain situation you might naturally gravitate towards expecting the worst and making negative assumptions.

Separation is an uncertain time, and if you assume that it will become ugly you will act protectively instinctively, and you could become defensive with you partner. This is problematic because in that situation you and your partner would not give one another the opportunity to act in good faith, and behave in an open, transparent way. Assume nothing.

Mistake #4: Communication breakdown: Communication is broadly defined as the sending or receiving of information, whether that's through writing, speaking or body language. There are two steps with communication: 1) the actual imparting of information, and 2) the receiving of the imparted information, i.e. the 'listening'.

At a particularly vulnerable and uncertain time, like separation, you and your partner do need to continue to communicate with one another—verbally or in writing—and you need to work at it. Communication breakdown leads to people disengaging with the process, which stops them from working as a team. This creates more of an opportunity for other people's opinions (and lawyers!) to become involved, which can be problematic.

If your partner appears put off or upset by what you've said to them, ask them, 'What did you hear when I said …' This will give you the opportunity to explain, and clarify if necessary, your intended message. Do the same for yourself, too. If you find yourself put off by something your partner has said, say, 'To clarify, you said X when I understood it to mean Y. Is that what you meant?'

Mistake #5: Listening to others: I'm sure you've heard the term 'misery enjoys company'. When it comes to separation, everyone knows someone who has been through a separation and 'it was the worst'. In listening to horror divorce stories, and potentially misguided advice from friends and family, you may be influenced to act in a way that is detrimental to your separation relationship. Put appropriate boundaries in place to manage other people's stories, thoughts and opinions so your decision-making ability isn't inappropriately interfered with.

Mistake #6: Having the wrong attitude: I'm a firm believer that what you put out into the universe, you get back. Behaving in a defensive and distrustful manner towards your partner will likely cause your relationship to deteriorate. Although you may both feel that your relationship is fundamentally flawed in some way, a positive attitude and the commitment to having a respectful separation will start you off on the right foot. Display a trusting, transparent manner, with good intentions.

Mistake #7: Deceit, dishonesty, omission: I've seen plenty of separations take a turn for the worse when people have lied, deceived, avoided or omitted information. Ninety-nine percent of the time, it doesn't end well. Sure, sometimes it's appropriate to omit bits and pieces of information, but at the end of the day, if the other person discovers the lie, omission or deceit, how are they going to feel when it comes to negotiating with you? Once the trust is gone, it's incredibly hard, laborious, time consuming and expensive to get it back. Honesty is the best policy in most situations.

Chapter 3

Momentum

In order to progress and finalise your separation, aside from you and your partner making it a priority, there needs to be momentum. As a colleague once said, both individuals need to be in a suspended state of discomfort in order to progress their separation because if either one becomes too comfortable with the situation they won't see the need to move on. The lack of progression, delay or feet dragging will just cause frustration and distrust.

It's safe to say that most couples don't aspire to have a long, drawn-out, expensive, nasty separation, preferring to be able to say that their separation was amicable and that their kids haven't been damaged or negatively impacted.

Momentum is about getting you and your partner on the same page, and setting a timeline for the tasks that you'll need to complete in order to reach an agreement.

You might be wondering about how to gain momentum if you, or your partner, are not at the acceptance stage yet, and the answer to that is, it's a balancing act. You've got to read the signs when it comes to your partner's behaviour. Are they feeling grief, or intentionally delaying and frustrating the separation process? Ask the same question of yourself: are you digging in your heels and intentionally delaying the separation? If so, maybe it's because you haven't yet come to terms with the relationship ending. Or you could be resisting the inevitable changes that will come because you're nervous and scared of the next steps.

At the end of the day, you and your partner can control how fast or slow your separation progresses and the amount of time it takes to get it finalised. Try to avoid overthinking and getting ahead of yourself. Just take one step at a time. I'll walk you through it.

In this chapter I will give you a summary of the financial documents you need to gather, and I will explain why you have to do this. I'll show you how to get on the same page as your partner about what will happen before you reach a final agreement. If you're following the AMICABLE method by yourself, I'll explain the things to consider so you can gain momentum. Lastly, I'll cover the issue of trust, and give you an example of a separating couple who made a few of the mistakes that I suggested in chapter 2 should be avoided.

Summary of financial documents

When it comes to agreeing about the split of the pie—your joint and separate assets, and debts and superannuation—you and your partner are under a legal obligation to provide full and frank financial disclosure. It doesn't matter if you think you won't be touching one another's stuff; you still have to disclose documents that show your financial position.

> **Legal jargon:** Disclosure is the exchange of documents that relate to your individual financial circumstances.

Why do you have to give your financial information to your partner and vice versa? Because the law says that in order for your agreement to be valid, legal and binding, you both have to provide full and frank financial disclosure.

But why? Because politicians (the law makers), courts, lawyers—and you and your partner—want to make sure that all cards are on the table when it comes to splitting the pie. Full disclosure means that you can enter into an agreement fully informed and you're aware of what you and your partner each walk away with at the end of the day in assets, debts, superannuation and resources.

At the end of this chapter I have provided a checklist of documents that you will need to put together to fulfil this obligation. In the spirit of momentum, nominate a date that you'll commit to getting the documents together. Make it no longer than three weeks.

If you and your partner are working through this book together, to help you get on the same page, schedule a date when you can do this together.

Getting on the same page

Separation can be scary. There can be so much uncertainty and insecurity that can cause fear, anger and self-doubt. When our environment is threatened, we typically kick into survival, protective mode. You're going to settle those fears by getting on the same page with your partner.

Having spent a few weeks getting your documents together, you and your partner will meet and work through the following steps. Then complete the same-page checklist at the end of the chapter.

Step 1: Start by exchanging your financial documents (the documents in the checklist).

Step 2: Take a blank piece of paper and draw a line down the middle of the page, creating two columns. At the top of the left-hand column, write 'Assets & Debts'. At the top of the right-hand column, write 'Estimated Value'. Then list all of the pie that's available to be split.

In the left-hand column, include all real estate, savings, cars, shares, motorbikes, tools, trailers and jewellery, plus any credit-card debts, other debts and personal loans you can think of. For now, ignore the value of each item.

If you prefer a more technological approach, you can download the free KickStarter Separation Pack from separatetogether.com.au/online-store/

Step 3: If you and your partner know for certain what each item is worth, or the amount owed on a debt because of the documents that you've exchanged, write down the value of each in the right-hand column. For example, you might know that you have an account balance of five hundred dollars because your bank statement says so. You'd then write $500 in the right hand column across from the corresponding line in the left hand column about savings.

Step 4: For assets like real estate, cars or shares, you'll need to agree on the steps you'll take to get an objective opinion about what the asset is worth. This will involve consulting a third person—preferably a professional, paid or unpaid—or finding out the market view of the value. You may have to do some research when it comes to market value, to determine what a buyer would pay for the item.

This is an important exercise to do together, because it's about the two of you working as a team and coming to a joint decision about what things are worth based on current independent evidence. A few suggestions that will help with this process:

- Cars and motorcycles: Visit RedBook to get a free appraisal. Simply insert the relevant vehicle details. The appropriate value to typically use is the midpoint of the private price guide. Consider whether to include any vehicle accessories and depreciation.

- Real estate: Get two to three appraisals from different real-estate agents to get a rough idea of what the property is worth. If there is an outlier (one that quotes a much higher or lower value than the others), consider getting another one or two appraisals, or simply get a formal, paid family-law valuation. This is where you ask a paid expert to prepare a report stating what they consider the property or properties are worth.
- Shares in publicly listed companies: Visit the company's website to find out the current value of each share. Also find a recent share-dividend member statement to identify the number of shares owned.
- Household contents: To work out the approximate value of tools, furniture or household contents have a look at Pickles Auctioneers or Gumtree. From a family-law perspective, the value to use is the 'fire sale' value.
- Interests in business: For businesses and companies in which you have an interest, speak with your accountant to find out the value of each enterprise.

Step 5: Now you're going to try and get as many runs on the board about mini agreements, which cover those things that will happen leading up to your final agreement:

- Leave or stay: Until you have a final agreement, there can be good reasons to stay in the house, and also leave the house. Your best option is to get specific advice before making a firm commitment to leave or stay.
- Living arrangements: Will one of you move out, or will you both continue to live under the same roof? Will this need to be revisited? If yes, when?
- Living expenses: Decide how you will pay for utilities, groceries, rates, insurances, rent/loan repayments, body corporate, internet, phone, car registration and insurances. Will the arrangement remain the same, be different, or need to be revisited?
- Salaries: Should you put both your salaries into a joint account, or redirect them into separate accounts?
- Debts: How will you pay loan, credit card and car-lease repayments?
- Withdrawal of funds: Do you need to speak with the bank about stopping the transfer or withdrawal of funds from any redraw facility, home-loan, credit card or joint savings account?
- Cardholders: Do you need to cancel any secondary cardholders or credit cards?
- Home-loan repayments: Should you switch your home-loan repayments from principal and interest, to interest only, or leave things as they are?

- Government benefits: Decide what will happen to government benefits such as family tax benefit A and/or B. Will you split the benefit(s), deposit it into a joint account, or arrange for it to be kept by one person?
- Review: Decide on timeframes for reviewing any of the mini agreements.
- If you have children together:
  - How will you share the children's care?
  - How will you pay for the children's expenses?
  - What will you tell your children, and when? Do you need or want help from a child psychologist or counsellor to work out what to say?
- Legal advice: Consider talking about whether to get legal advice, and if so when. The majority of separating couples I work with actively try to avoid using lawyers. Understandably, they're concerned that lawyers will interfere and encourage the other partner to go for more, causing them to fight it out in court with expensive legal fees.

When lawyers give advice, they provide it on the basis of one person's version of facts only. Legal advice can therefore be different for each partner. One thing you can do to minimise any differences in the legal advice you both receive is to come up with a statement of facts: information about the relationship.

You can download the free KickStarter Separation Pack from separatetogether.com.au/online-store/ It contains a questionnaire that you and your partner can complete. Your answers might be the same or different, but you can then take that completed document to your separate lawyers and receive advice on what you say are the facts, as well as what your partner says are the facts.

It's also important to understand that you don't have to sign up with a lawyer and engage them to act for you. You can simply ask them to provide you with legal advice and nothing more.

The list above is simply to give you some ideas to think about. You needn't reach an agreement on everything. Write down, in dot-point format, any mini agreements. Getting written or verbal confirmation of these agreements will demonstrate to both of you that you're capable of reaching an agreement together, thereby giving you confidence in your ability to reach a final agreement together.

Step 6: Complete the Next Steps plan and follow through.

CHAPTER 3: MOMENTUM

Gaining momentum solo

If you are not working through this book with your partner and intend to progress your separation on your own as much as possible, then, word to the wise, you may not need to explicitly confirm with your partner these mini agreements. The need or desire to do this will depend on what you could gain or lose by having that discussion with your partner.

Is your partner likely to assume (as you are) that things will continue the same until you reach a final agreement? Will they withdraw their financial support? Will they take the children?

Instead of having this mini-agreement discussion, you could try to nudge the separation along by making suggestions for getting those objective third-party evidence appraisals done together, and providing your partner with your financial documents. Or you could exchange your individual financial documents at the same time, and after that put together a breakdown of the pie.

I recommend getting legal advice to find out what is your best next step. I know I sound like a lawyer when I say this, but there could be strategic decisions that could benefit or disadvantage you.

A question of trust

This part relates to the level of trust you have in your partner, and whether or not you believe there is a need to act to protective yourself. What do you need to mindful of? Do you need to change any of your passwords? Do you need to redirect any of your mail? Do you need to remove your partner from your credit card, or remove yourself from theirs? Do you need to talk to the bank about freezing any of your savings, or make changes to redraw facilities or offset accounts?

One of my clients discovered, after separation, that her husband had transferred the entire balance of their joint bank account, which was about $30,000, into an account in his own name. My client was shocked and distressed by her husband's actions, and was understandably distrustful of him.

The husband had engaged a collaboratively trained lawyer, who spoke with him about returning the funds to the joint bank account, and making a stipulation that the transfer of further funds required joint signatures.

The husband claimed that he hadn't intended to upset his wife, but he had 'heard from friends' that he should transfer all the money so his wife 'couldn't get it'. His intention had been to act protectively towards himself, but his unilateral action caused a rift and it took a lot of work and effort to get the separation relationship back on track so things could proceed in a constructive way.

This is a good example of mistakes not to make. The husband listened to friends and then acted unilaterally; his actions were not transparent when it came to communicating with his wife.

Documents checklist

The following covers the different types of information (documents) you and your partner will be required to give to one another:

- *Information about your income:* This means anything that is paid to you, or a trust, company, partnership or corporation in which you have an interest in, or income you allocate to someone else. Collect your payslips for the last three pay cycles. Also your individual tax returns and notices of assessment for the last three financial years, as well as for any trust, company and/or corporation in which you have an interest. In addition, any share dividend statements.
- *Current superannuation entitlement balance:* This can be your superannuation member statement for each fund in which you have an interest. For

defined benefit-scheme interests—public sector superannuation (PSS), commonwealth sector superannuation (CSS), military super, and defence force retirement and death benefits scheme (DFRDB)—you also need what's called a formal family law valuation.

- *Self-managed superfund:* If you are a member of a self-managed superfund, a copy of the trust deed, and the three most recent financial statements for the fund.
- *Corporate interest:* If you have an interest in a corporation, financial statements for the last three financial years, including balance sheets, profit-and-loss accounts, depreciation schedules, and taxation returns; a copy of the corporation's constitution and any amendments; and a document identifying the directors and shareholders (I suggest getting an ASIC search performed).
- *Trust interest:* If you have an interest in a trust—either as an appointer or trustee, or as an eligible beneficiary to the capital or income, or your child or partner is an eligible beneficiary—a copy of the financial statements for the last three financial years, including balance sheets, profit and loss accounts, depreciation schedules and taxation returns; and a copy of the trust deed, including amendments.

- *Business interest:* If you have an interest in a business, any business-activity statements for the previous twelve months.
- *Partnership interest:* If you have an interest in a partnership, a copy of the financial statements for the three most recent financial years, including balance sheets, profit and loss accounts, depreciation schedules and taxation returns; and a copy of the partnership agreement, including any amendments.
- *Bank accounts:* Documents (bank statements) showing the balance of accounts.
- *Debts owing:* Documents showing the amount of any debts owed (bank statements, hire-purchase lease agreement/payout figure).

Same-page checklist		
We met on (date):		
We exchanged our financial documents:	☐ Yes	☐ No
We need to exchange additional information:	☐ Yes	☐ No
The following information still needs to be exchanged: *Next to each point, write the name of the person who is to provide the information	1. 2. 3. 4. 5. 6.	

Action Tasks

Task:		Name of person responsible:
Arrange for appraisal(s) on real estate		
Name of agent 1:		
Name of agent 2:		
Name of agent 3:		
Arrange for vehicle appraisals		
Vehicle 1 (make):		
Vehicle 2 (make):		
Vehicle 3 (make):		

Other:

Tick which of these are relevant:

- ☐ Speak with bank/mortgage broker about borrowing capacity
- ☐ Enquire about mediation services (cost, availability)
- ☐ Enquire about child psychologist (cost, availability)
- ☐ Speak with an accountant
- ☐ Speak with the bank

Comments:

Next-steps plan

We will meet again on/about (date):	
We will meet at (location):	

Chapter 4
Interests

According to the Family Court of Australia's 2018 annual report, 28,590 Australians reached an agreement together about their financial split and/or their children's care arrangements, and submitted their agreement paperwork to the court to be signed off on without stepping foot inside a courtroom. (Along the way, they also probably sorted out arrangements for maintenance, financial support for any children, and finalising their divorce).

Does that come as a surprise?

The couples that successfully reach an agreement together are able to do so because they think of the big picture. They keep things high level, with their eye on the prize. They don't spend (much) time and energy discussing and disagreeing on comparatively smaller, insignificant issues, like who gets the $350 coffee machine or the white serving platter you got as a wedding gift from your mum's next-door neighbour. They don't sweat the small stuff.

As they say, marriage is grand: divorce can be a hundred grand, and the emotional stress and pain can be, as MasterCard says, 'priceless'.

In this chapter I will cover your interests and concerns, and I will show you how to get your priorities in order so you and your partner can also be one of those successful couples that reaches an agreement together without stepping foot in a courtroom.

Your interests and concerns

Grab some paper and a pen, and you need a timer so also grab your phone or a stopwatch This initial twenty-minute exercise, which you'll do alone, will help you get perspective on the big picture, gearing you up for your agreement discussion with your partner later on. Forget spelling and punctuation, you're going to spend the next seven minutes furiously writing out what your interests are.

Your interests aren't your hobbies; they're what you identify as your concerns, needs, priorities and goals. Using Abraham Maslow's well-known hierarchy of needs, the two basic categories of human needs can be summarised as those physiological (food, water, sleep, warmth) and safety (shelter, control, economic security, physical and psychological safety).

Think of the specific needs that you need ticked in order to achieve an acceptable agreement outcome.

Step 1: Take your stopwatch, or open your phone and bring up your timer. Allocate yourself seven minutes, or even fifteen minutes, and press start. Get writing about every single thought that comes to mind when you think about what your interests are. Here are a few ideas to get you started:
- I need financial stability and security.
- I need to be as financially independent as possible. I'm worried about how I can afford to live. I need certainty about my living expenses and income.
- I worry about being able to rebuild my life financially.

- I'm close to retirement. I need to have financial security for my future.
- Our financial split should reflect what I brought into the relationship. I need our financial split to reflect the inheritance I received during the relationship.
- I need to do further study and achieve qualifications in order to re-establish my career and re-enter the workforce.
- The kids need stability when it comes to their care and where they live.
- My time out of the workforce while I raised the kids should be reflected in the financial settlement.
- My partner and I need to reach an agreement so I can move on.
- I hope my partner and I get on so we can be effective co-parents for our kids.
- At the end of the day, I want my partner and I to be friends.
- It's important to me that the kids are privately educated.
- The kids should have the same opportunities they would have had if we were still together.
- We should both contribute to the cost of the care of the kids, whether it's the same amount or differing proportions.
- We should both contribute to the medical costs for our kids.

- We need a financial plan for our kids for when they leave school.

Done it? Brilliant! The exercise you've just done can be a hard one to do, which is why I gave you some ideas. You're going to need to revisit this list and work on it over time because you'll recognise during this process that there are other needs, concerns and goals that you'd ideally like to achieve.

Step 2: For the next part of this exercise, you're going to spend three minutes going through your list and crossing out anything that's attached to a specific outcome. For example, if you've written 'I want the house' or 'I want to keep my super' cross it out because it's a specific outcome that you want.

If you go into the agreement discussion with your partner with specific outcomes that you want, you risk going in being positional. You will measure each and every option that you both come up with against the specific outcome that you've identified, causing you to be closed minded and not open to alternative possibilities or creative outcomes that have the potential to meet both of your needs. So set the timer for three minutes and go!

Step 3: The third and final part of this exercise is to write down, next to each need that you've identified, your *why*. This will require you to reflect on why each need you've identified is important to you and what it means. Understanding and knowing your *why* will help you in communicating your interests to your partner (which I cover in detail later on). Most of us are more accepting of an opinion, decision or outcome if we're given reasons.

If you want to take it one step further—and I suggest you do—step into your partner's shoes. If you were in their position, what would you be most concerned about? What would you need, prioritise and want as a goal? Why do you think those things would be important to you if you were your partner? Stepping into your partner's shoes will help you in your agreement discussion when it comes to understanding their perspective.

Chapter 5
Consider your Backup Plan

To have the best opportunity for success in reaching a final agreement, you and your partner need to prepare for your agreement discussion. As part of this preparation, you're going to consider your backup plan if you don't reach a final agreement together.

We're frequently offered products that intend to provide peace of mind in the event of potential what-if worst-case scenarios, for example, comprehensive car, funeral, building, home and contents, life and income protection insurances. By having these insurances in place, we have some peace of mind and feel reassured that if the worst-case scenario happens, we've got some protection or compensation available to us.

Consider your backup plan as your insurance against you agreeing to an outcome that you should refuse because it compromises or doesn't satisfactorily meet your interests (Fisher & Ury, 2012, p. 99).

Throughout this book, I've used the term 'agreement discussion', which means the negotiation you and your partner undertake to reach a final agreement together, whether that's parenting, the financial split, child support, or maintenance. I've used this term because I believe it's a nicer, softer term to use than 'negotiation'. It's been commonly said that the most powerful position in any negotiation is the ability to walk away. In doing so, you are making a decision to pursue other, presumably better, alternatives than what is being put forward in the negotiation.

While the focus of this chapter is on the financial split after separation, you can also use these principles to reach an agreement about parenting, maintenance and child support.

So, you're going to have an agreement discussion with your partner to reach a final agreement together. Before having that agreement discussion, you're going to consider your backup plan: what will happen if you don't reach a final agreement? Don't worry; I will hold your hand while you work this out. You're going to work out your backup plan even before you have your agreement discussion. It's part of the preparation.

In this chapter I discuss in detail the importance of having a backup plan. I show you how to develop your backup plan so that you can walk into your agreement discussion with the confidence of knowing that you have the ability to walk away without compromising your interests. This is probably the biggest *doing* chapter in the book. I can't stress how important it is for you to develop and consider your backup plan, not only practically but also psychologically.

Your backup plan

First we start with the agreement discussion. In any setting, the purpose of negotiation is to achieve a better outcome than if you don't negotiate. The idea of having a (financial) backup plan is to stop you from falling into the trap of accepting an outcome that's wrong for you, either because you've been worn down and are giving in, you want to avoid confrontation, or you prioritise remaining on good terms with your partner to your detriment, thereby compromising your interests.

In their international bestseller, *Getting to Yes: Negotiating an Agreement Without Giving In*, Roger Fisher and William Ury (2012) coined the BATNA concept, which stands for 'best alternative to a negotiated agreement'. They describe the BATNA as a plan to develop regarding the steps that a party can act on if a final agreement isn't reached.

To put this into context, your backup plan isn't to go and see a lawyer to fight it out in court if you and your partner don't agree. It's more practical than that. In the context of your financial split, it's actually the decision about what you'll do with your property, debts and superannuation until such time as you reach a final agreement.

Let me give you an example.

Jack and Kath own a house together. At the moment, neither of them can afford to refinance the home loan and pay out to the other person an appropriate amount in order to keep the house. They know that it's a bad time in the market to sell, as property values have dropped and they'd lose thousands of dollars. Instead of one of them keeping the house and making a less than reasonable payment to the other, which doesn't satisfy either of their interests, Jack and Kath agree that they'll rent out the house and revisit reaching a final agreement outcome in twelve months' time.

In tabling their final agreement for twelve months' time, neither Jack nor Kath have compromised their interests. They're both prepared to carry the risk of getting in tenants, and the market improving or not, rather than incur financial losses. For both of them, their backup plan is more attractive to them than the alternative of selling the house at a loss, or accepting less of a payment than is reasonable if one of them kept it.

Let me give you another example.

Jo and Keith have separated. They have two kids together. Jo and the kids continue to live in the family home. Keith recently moved out. Jo is concerned about their separation affecting the kids. It's important to her that she and Keith continue to co-parent effectively and minimise any conflict. She wants the children to continue to be brought up in a healthy, happy, stable environment, and have a positive relationship with both her and Keith.

Jo feels that she needs to be in a position to own a house. Why? Because as far as she's concerned, ownership of a home symbolises her ability to provide long-term stability for their kids.

Jo and Keith are meeting for the agreement discussion. Jo hasn't thought about a backup plan if she and Keith can't reach a final agreement. After some brainstorming together about all of the different agreement outcomes, Keith suggests that they sell the family home and split the sale proceeds in different proportions. Jo realises that the amount she'd receive from the sale proceeds wouldn't give her enough for a deposit on a property she'd have to rent for at least two years and save.

Keith suggests another proposal: Jo keeps the family home and pays him out. On her income, Jo knows that she can't afford to pay Keith the amount he wants—which she feels is reasonable—as well as refinance the home loan into her own name.

With no back up plan in mind, Jo feels that she is left with no option but to agree with Keith's proposal in order to finalise the separation. Jo reluctantly agrees to sell the family home and split the sale proceeds.

Imagine if before going into the agreement discussion, Jo had thought of a back up plan and her backup plan was for her and the kids to continue to live in the family home, without Keith.

Jo would then have been in a position to assess Keith's proposals against this back up plan to determine the most attractive option, thereby minimising the risk of her compromising her interests. Additionally, Jo could've then workshopped Keith's proposal that she keep the family home and pay him out. The issue simply came down to

Jo's immediate ability to be able to afford to refinance the existing home loan into her own name and pay Keith out.

Joe and Keith could've workshopped the back up plan as an option, whereby Jo pay to Keith the agreed amount but in instalments over a period of time.

Doing so would've satisfied Keith's need of a cash payment to enable him to re-establish himself financially, and satisfied Jo's interests in owning a home to provide stability for the kids and presumably maintaining the effective co-parenting relationship with Keith.

The importance of a backup plan

You are now going into the agreement discussion with the ability to compare proposals to your backup plan and work out which appeals to you more, thereby minimising the risk of you compromising your interests. You're not going in positional, with a specific outcome that you want, or with a closed mind. There is no bottom line or buffer for what you're willing to accept or not. Psychologically knowing that you have a well thought through tentative backup plan about what you'll do if you don't reach a final agreement can give you that extra oomph of confidence when or if you decide to walk away from the agreement discussion.

What your backup plan should cover

You'll remember that in the chapter on momentum, you did an exercise about getting you and your partner on the same page. You reached mini agreements about day-to-day issues, where you'll both be living, how living expenses for the family will get paid, and how debts will be paid until you have the agreement discussion.

And it's typical that people are able to reach an agreement on these things as well as what I call 'the noise'. The noise consists of peripheral matters such as how you will divide the household contents, deciding who keeps which car, and what will happen to any shares, businesses or companies.

You might not need to come up with a backup plan for specific mini issues, just the big-ticket items. In my experience, there are usually two or three issues that need to be agreed upon. A few examples of possible big-ticket issues:

- If person A is keeping the house, should there be a payment to person B? If yes, what should that amount be?
- If the house is to be sold, how should the sale proceeds be split between person A and person B?
- Should there be a super split? If yes, how should that super be split between person A and person B?

CHAPTER 5: CONSIDER YOUR BACKUP PLAN

You'll learn in the next chapter about the approach and principles that the law considers to be relevant when working out what is a fair split of the pie. But for people trying to work it out themselves, it comes down to their financial ability, and what they feel is morally fair when considering any cash injections or gifts either of them has received during the relationship, or the kids' future care arrangements and any impact that will have.

So the answer to the question about whether you should have more than one backup plan really depends on what things you and your partner have been unable to reach a final agreement on: whether it's the big ticket items or the mini issues. Remember, this is your alternative to a final agreement—what will happen until that final agreement is reached.

As an example of a mini issue, it might be a situation where you can't afford to pay or contribute towards the personal loan or lease repayments for a car. Your backup plan might look like this:

- Sell the car and pay out the debt.
- Propose that your partner takes the car and pay the debt repayments, with the car to be transferred into your partner's name later on when your separation is official and you have reached a final agreement.

- Continue to drive the car, but propose that your partner take over the debt repayments.

When it comes to the big-ticket item of real estate, your options might look like this: you live in the house, you move out, your partner moves in, you rent the house, or you sell the house. There are many options available to you.

Developing your backup plan

In any negotiation 'the better your BATNA, the greater your power' (Fisher & Ury 2012, p. 104). Now we'll cover what steps you need to take to ensure you have that power.

Step 1: Grab your pen and some blank paper. At the top of the page, write out this sentence: 'If we don't reach an agreement together about our financial split, then …'

Step 2: Draw a vertical line down the middle of the page so there are two columns. On the left-hand side, write down your backup plan in response to what you will do if you don't reach an agreement on the big-ticket items and those mini issues that conceivably might not get resolved on an interim basis.

Step 3: On the right-hand side, across from your backup plan, write the reasons justifying your backup plan. These reasons could be financial, or based on advice you've received.

Step 4: In a different coloured pen, write down all of the criticisms that your partner could make in response to your backup plan. Then write down your comment or response to those potential criticisms.

Step 5: Grab another piece of paper. At the top of the page, write down, 'If we don't reach a final agreement together, my partner's backup plan could be …' Then write down what you consider your partner's backup plan might be. Get into their shoes and think about the reasons why they might want their backup plan.

What to do with your backup plan

When your backup plan is written down, take it with you to your agreement discussion with your partner. You needn't show them your backup plan. When you're having the agreement discussion, you'll be assessing which of the proposals is more appealing to you: your backup plan, or your partner's proposed outcome (Fisher & Ury 2012, p 104).

If your backup plan is more appealing to you, you're essentially protecting yourself against agreeing to an outcome that doesn't fulfil your interests in the way it should.

It's not about saying no to the proposed outcome but rather seeing if you can improve the proposed outcome so you and your partner's interests can be satisfied such that you prefer the workshopped proposed outcome than your back up plan (Fisher & Ury 2012, p. 72).

Chapter 6
Advice

I magine this scenario some way in the future. (Or perhaps this has happened to you in the past.) You subscribe to a dating service. You are matched with someone who appears quite attractive in their profile picture, but when you meet them in person you discover that the photo was taken more than a decade ago and they're not quite so attractive now. You're definitely not interested. You probably feel like you've wasted your time.

It's frustrating to deal with people who aren't real, either because they don't know *how* to be real or they're incapable of it because they're a bit delusional. Getting real about your own expectations is therefore a must to ensure you're not that person with the decade-old profile photo. The benefit of getting a reality check by speaking with a professional is that when you have the agreement discussion with your partner, you can cut through the rubbish and have a productive discussion about potential realistic agreement outcomes.

In this chapter I will explain what the law says in general terms about splitting the pie, maintenance after separation, and care arrangements for children and child support. I'll discuss the importance of choosing the right lawyer, and also the other professionals you should consider approaching for advice.

Splitting the pie after separation

The law says that after separation there are four steps involved in working out what's an appropriate split of the pie.

Step 1: What are the assets, debts, superannuation and financial resources that make up the pie?

Step 2: What are the contributions to the pie made by each person, or on their behalf, or their child's behalf?

CHAPTER 6: ADVICE

Step 3: What are each person's future needs?
Step 4: Is the proposed split of the pie 'just and equitable'?

Step 1: Work out the complete pie that's available to be split between you and your partner. In completing the exercise in chapter 3 you will have this information. Combine all of the assets, debts and superannuation that are in your joint or separate names, and their values. Lawyers call this the non-superannuation pool and the superannuation pool.

If either you or your partner are the beneficiary of a trust, or have a pending court claim where there is the potential for a financial payout, then this is relevant to the pie and can be considered. Inheritances can be considered relevant to the pie if they're about to be distributed, or the person gifting the inheritance has lost the capacity to change their will.

If you separated more than twelve months ago, or the pie now is now different to what it was when you separated (for example, you or your partner might have sold a property, incurred large debts or acquired more assets), you can make two separate lists identifying the pie as it is at the current date, and the date of separation but be aware that the correct legal approach is to work out what the pie is now. This is because the law recognises that you and your partner may have contributed in different ways to today's pie that could go unrecognised, and therefore be unfair, if the pie was split using the separation date.

Step 2: Work out how you and your partner contributed to the pie. Consider financial, non-financial, homemaker and parenting contributions. Based on the contributions made by you and your partner, there could be a swing in one person's favour over the other to say that one of you made the greater contribution to the pie.

Think about the ways in which you have both contributed to the pie:

- What was the value of any savings, vehicles, shares, real-estate equity, debt or superannuation that you and your partner had when you started living together or got married, whichever occurred first?
- If the relationship was short, say seven years or less, what were your individual incomes during the relationship over the years?
- Did you or your partner receive any lump-sum financial gifts, inheritance or windfall during the

relationship or after separation? If so, when was it received? What did you or your partner do with the funds?
- If you have kids, either together or from a previous relationship, how was the parenting role carried out? Did you both perform equal roles, or did one person do more of the parenting?
- If either of you have children from a previous relationship, how were or are they financially supported?
- How have you and your partner directly or indirectly financially contributed (even if someone has done so on your or your child's behalf) to the 'acquisition, conservation or improvement of any of the property' in joint or separate names?
- How have you and your partner directly or indirectly contributed in a non-financial way (even if someone has done so on your or your child's behalf) to the 'acquisition, conservation or improvement of any of the property' in your joint or separate names?
- How have you and your partner contributed to the welfare of the family, including in the capacity of homemaker or parent (non-financial contributions)?

> Non-financial domestic contributions that are considered in a separation: cooking, washing, cleaning, ironing, grocery shopping, looking after children, manual labour, improvements to the family home, repairs, general maintenance, and gardening.

Step 3: Consider your separate future needs. This is relevant to whether one partner needs to receive more the pie now in recognition of being impacted financially because of their future needs. There are many factors that can be considered, for both you and your partner:

- Your respective ages and state of health
- Your respective incomes, separate property, and available financial resources
- Your respective physical and mental capacity to obtain appropriate gainful employment
- Care arrangements for a child or children of the relationship under eighteen years
- Your individual commitments to support yourselves, a child or children, or another person you have a duty to maintain
- Your or your partner's responsibilities to support any other person

- Your or your partner's eligibility to a government pension, benefit or allowance, and the corresponding rate
- A standard of living that 'in all the circumstances is reasonable'
- The duration of the relationship and the extent to which it has affected the earning capacity of either of you
- The need to protect the parent who wishes to continue in that role
- If either of you is living with another person, the financial circumstances relating to the cohabitation
- The level of child support you or your partner have provided or may be liable to provide to the other
- Any other circumstances that need to be taken into account by the court to ensure the justice of the case

Step 4: This final step is where an assessment is made as to whether the overall proposed split of the pie, with the adjustments at steps two and three, as the case may be, is 'just and equitable'? There can be an adjustment to make the overall division fair.

Australia's family-law legislation, although outdated in some respects, is intended to be a framework that cohesively reflects our community's socially accepted values and standards. Society recognises that people can make valuable contributions to the family unit that are not necessarily always financial.

How can you work out what is a fair split of the pie? The short answer is that you can't unless you speak with an experienced family lawyer or trawl through reported case law decisions and then interpret, understand and correctly apply the principles to your circumstances.

When it comes to applying the law to the facts of a case to determine an appropriate split, judges have discretion, with restrictions. If you speak with a lawyer, they'll likely give you a range of (around 10% depending on the circumstances) what could be an appropriate outcome, for example saying that an appropriate outcome may be for you to receive 'between 55 and 65 percent'.

Maintenance (alimony)

Maintenance is financial support (or not) to one person after separation. It's relevant where one partner has a shortfall between their income and reasonable expenditure, and the other partner has a buffer between their income and reasonable expenditure.

Maintenance is calculated by working out a person's income (excluding child support and any Centrelink or government benefits, pension or allowance) and the average weekly expenditure that relates to them personally. Maintenance is separate to child support and is generally separate from the split of the pie.

The care of children

What does the law say about parenting after separation? The law says that after separation, arrangements for children should be in the child's best interests. There are two primary considerations, known as 'the twin pillars', when working out what is in a child's best interests: the benefit of a child having a meaningful relationship with both their parents, and the need to protect a child from harm.

There are a bunch of additional factors that may be considered, including the child's view (allowing for their age, level of understanding and maturity), the degree of participation by both parents in the child's life, each parent's attitude towards parenting, and their ability to provide for the child's needs. It also covers fulfilment of parental obligations, including financial and major long-term decision-making, and the relevance of any family-violence allegations. This list isn't exhaustive.

> There is no presumption that 50/50 care is in a child's best interests. Your children's ages and what their care arrangements have been during the relationship and since separation are important to the decision about their living arrangements.

I've had clients who have had success with their children living in shared-care arrangements (which is defined as a child living with a parent for five nights or more per fortnight), where the kids are of school age and the parents are able to communicate well enough with one another to prioritise the children and have an effective co-parenting relationship.

The object of parenting legislation is to ensure that the best interests of children are met by promoting and ensuring (with some caveats) that they have the benefit of meaningful involvement with their parents, they're protected from harm, they receive adequate and proper parenting to 'help them achieve their full potential', and parents fulfil their duties and carry out their responsibilities.

There are two common big-ticket matters that parents are most concerned with when it comes to parenting their children after separation: parental responsibility (long-term decision-making), and appropriate care arrangements, which could mean the children split their time between two parents/households.

Parental responsibility: This means 'all the duties, powers, responsibilities and authority which, by law, parents have in relation to children'. Breaking this down, it means that as you and your partner brought a child into the world together, you automatically have shared parental responsibility. You don't have to get a court order for this.

'Parental responsibility', as defined by law, is distinct from 'day-to-day parental responsibility'. Day-to-day responsibility covers those decisions a parent makes when their child is in their care, for example, what the child eats, what they wear, whether they go to school if they're sick. Parental responsibility has more to do with long-term decisions such as religion, schooling, education and health.

You and your partner can agree to have equal shared parental responsibility, which means that you both have an equal say and you share in all proposed decisions that may affect your child's long-term care, welfare and development. You or your partner can have sole parental responsibility in relation to some parenting aspects, or all if you both agree.

Appropriate care arrangements: When it comes to your kids and working out what's best for them, you're generally going to be the expert albeit with some restrictions. You'll likely know your child's personality, traits and quirks. Part of deciding what's in your child's best interests is considering these things, but it's also understanding their developmental (emotional, intellectual and psychological) needs with regard to their age, and the quality of their relationship with you and the other parent. A child expert can give insight into these matters.

In a research report by Caruana, Ferro, Smyth, Weston, Whitfield, Wolcott and Qu (2004) key findings are made about successful post separation care arrangements for children, particularly for shared care (which is about five nights per fortnight):

- Parents living close to one another
- Parents being flexible, accommodating and committing to making the shared parenting arrangement work
- Parents respecting one another's competencies as parents and having appropriate parental capability and skills
- Quality of the relationship between the children and each parent
- Environmental resources, such as appropriate housing and income, financial independence
- Work flexibility and family-friendly work practices
- Parents having a civil or businesslike relationship
- Parents having a child-focused approach to their parenting

Caruana et al. (2004) also notes that infants and pre-school age children 'are likely to have a stronger psychological attachment to one parent' (Caruana et al. 2004, p. 118) which should be taken into account when considering their living arrangements.

> Would your child's views be considered? It comes down to how old your child is and their level of maturity. A child expert—psychologist, psychiatrist or an appropriately qualified counsellor—is able to express a view on the degree of weight that should be attached to any views expressed by your children when it comes to where they want to live and when they want to see each parent.

Child support

The law says that you and your child's other parent have a legal duty to maintain your child, otherwise known as child support. Using a formula, the Department of Human Services Child-Support Agency (CSA) calculates the child support that you or your partner are required to pay to the other parent, which is based on three things: income for you and your partner, your children's ages, and the number of overnights that your children are in your care and your partner's care.

You can get a free, anonymous estimate of how much you or your partner may be assessed to pay or what you are entitled to receive by visiting the CSA's website for the online child support estimator https://processing.csa.gov.au/estimator/About.aspx.

In some circumstances, parents agree that in order to give their children more opportunities, or to provide for them meaningfully, there needs to be a greater amount of financial support than the assessed amount. They may therefore agree that the parent assessed to pay child support pays a higher amount. Or they may agree that one or both parents contribute—whether in the same amount or differing proportions—towards their children's non-periodic expenses, for example, school fees, uniforms, extracurricular activities, private health insurances, and out-of-pocket medical expenses.

Child support is generally separate to the financial split and maintenance. You can make an application to the CSA immediately after separation for a formal child-support assessment. There can be reasons why it might not be in your interests to do so, though. For example, the amount that your partner may be formally assessed to pay might be less than the level of financial support they're currently paying or have agreed to pay. Consider getting advice from a lawyer on what to do about this.

Choosing the right lawyer

Are you worried that if you meet with a lawyer for advice you will end up in court with a big legal bill? That's enough to put me off seeing a lawyer, too. I believe that, like eggs, when it comes to lawyers there are good ones and there are bad ones. One of the biggest mistakes I see people make when separating is seeing the wrong kind of lawyer.

The wrong kind of lawyer: You can work out what a lawyer is like by having a brief phone chat with them, reading their profile on the firm's website, checking out their social media, and reading blogs if they've written any. If the language is legalese, they talk about going to court from the get-go, you can't work out their message, or you don't think you'd click with them, they may not be the right kind of lawyer for you.

The right kind of lawyer: I believe that the kind of lawyer you want to be speaking to is collaboratively trained; they've undergone additional voluntary training to make them better at helping separating families stay out of court and reach an agreement together. Also, you want them to be experienced in family law. By this I mean that they don't just dabble in family law; their primary or whole practice is based in family law.

As an experienced family lawyer, they'll know the ropes and how judges interpret the law. They apply non-legal skills, such as empathy and insight, and give appropriate legal advice. They talk about goals and priorities, and align those with realisable outcomes that don't involve going to court.

There are collaborative family-law practice groups all around Australia, consisting of like-minded family lawyers, financial planners/advisors, mediators, psychologists and other professionals who work with separating families. Simply Google 'collaborative family law [*insert state/territory*]' and your local practice group will likely appear.

Your reasons for speaking with a lawyer are many:

- Receive specific advice about how the law applies to you, whether it's about the split of your finances, or parenting, maintenance and child support
- Get a reality check on your expectations
- Get advice on the pitfalls and benefits of any agreement you and your partner may already have
- Find a lawyer who can act on your behalf if you want or need them to
- Workshop different financial-split outcomes and give an opinion on what your next steps should be
- Find out the legal information that is relevant to you

Ideally, you want to have your eyes wide open to any agreement that you make. This includes knowing the advantages and disadvantages of the agreement, whether the law says it's an appropriate outcome, any potential difficulties in implementing and enforcing it, and your rights, obligations and entitlements according to the law.

Mortgage broker

A mortgage broker is basically the middleman or woman between you (as a borrower) and the bank (as a lender) for big money lending for real estate. They're familiar with the lending requirements of each bank and effectively do the legwork in finding the best loan for their client.

Mortgage brokers do get a financial kickback (commission) from the bank that their client signs with, which is typically for the duration of their loan with the bank. The client pays nothing up front to the mortgage broker. Benefits of using a mortgage broker:

- Save time by having a professional who knows what they're doing find the best loan deal for you
- Shave potentially thousands of dollars off your home loan
- Find out your borrowing capacity, and your ability to comply with any financial-split agreement reached
- An obligation-free arrangement means that if you decide to opt to refinance with your existing bank

you've merely used up two hours or so of your life; a good mortgage broker will tell you to remain with your bank if that's the best deal going

A numbers professional

The 2015 Australian Psychological Society Stress and Wellbeing in Australia survey identified that financial issues are rated as the top cause of stress, with 49 percent of people surveyed identifying personal finances as their top cause. In a 2011 survey carried out by Relationships Australia, 71 percent of respondents indicated that financial stress was more likely to push them apart from their partner than keep them together.

With this in mind, you don't want to over commit yourself financially after separation. A numbers professional (accountant, financial advisor or financial planner) can give you a reality check. They will look at your ability to service a home loan on your income with your expenditure, and demonstrate what your life could look like if, for example, as a condition of your agreement you received cash instead of splitting superannuation.

A numbers professional can offer advice on how to re-establish yourself financially after separation, including saving for a house deposit or planning for retirement. They can explain the relevance of insurance, help you plan for payment of your children's education and expenses, and advise you on wealth protection, bankruptcy, asset finance and commercial loans, capital gains and division 7A tax issues, and business valuations.

Child experts

Child psychology is the study of child development from birth to adolescence. Lawyers typically aren't qualified to give an expert opinion on your child's developmental needs, but they can give you advice on the application of the law to parenting matters. For example, a lawyer can advise on what the law says about parenting after separation, strategy, and what judges may determine to be an appropriate outcome with regard to your circumstances, but they can't talk specifics about the psychology aside from what they read and learn.

Judges consider and give weight to recommendations made by child experts to help them determine what is in a child's best interests. Child psychologists, psychiatrists or appropriately qualified and experienced counsellors are the experts who can help you and your partner work out what is in your children's best interests without going to court, and this will help you with your parenting agreement discussion.

Chapter 7

Brainstorm

This is the skinniest chapter in this book because there's little to know other than that you need to do it. If you're anything like me, you might have a head-down-bum-up approach to work and life. Maybe like me you're more about getting things done and not stuffing around. You might think that a brainstorming exercise is 'fluffy'. If so, you might be surprised to learn that collaboratively trained family lawyers across Australia, and internationally, get their clients to brainstorm all potential agreement outcomes to help couples reach agreements together.

In the context of your separation, the purpose of a brainstorming exercise is to produce ideas that have the potential to solve the problem of reaching an agreement that satisfies both of your interests as much as possible. It could be an agreement on the split of the pie; suitable arrangements for your children's care; or future financial support for you, your partner or your children.

How to brainstorm

Brainstorming is a fairly simple and fast exercise. When you and your partner sit down to have your agreement discussion, you'll write down on some butcher's paper or a whiteboard every single potential agreement outcome that you come up with. Assuming that you're both focused on interests and not specific outcomes, you should be able to come up with loads of options within a few minutes.

Your focus should be on producing ideas about the potential agreement outcomes. It's not about judging whether they're good or bad ideas, or whether you both like them or not (Fisher & Ury 2012, p. 62). If you spend more than ten minutes doing this exercise and come up with less than ten options, go back to the drawing board and do it again.

Here is an example I came up with in one minute.

Jack and Jill own a house, two cars and shares, and they both have superannuation. They brainstorm the following options:

- One person keeps the house and pays out the other person
- One person keeps the house and there is no payment to the other person
- Sell the house and divide the sale proceeds between them
- Each person keeps their own car
- They swap their cars
- They sell their cars
- They split the shares between them
- They sell the shares and divide the sale proceeds between them
- One person keeps the shares
- They keep their own superannuation
- One person gives some of their superannuation to the other person

In the next chapter you'll learn what to do with your brainstormed ideas using the LEADR-to-yes model.

Chapter 8
LEADR to Yes

Ah, the agreement discussion also referred to as 'the negotiation'. You might be wondering where on earth do you start. How do you and your partner have a constructive, productive conversation together to reach an agreement? What do you say to each other? What do you avoid saying? Should a lawyer or other third person be involved?

In my years of practice as a family lawyer, I've discovered that separating couples can struggle to know how to effectively and productively talk to one another to reach an agreement, which brings me to my LEADR-to-yes model.

I know that when this acronymic is read aloud it sounds like 'lead her to yes', but gentlemen, that's not the case. It's not a gender-specific method. LEADR-to-yes is a process I've created that will give all couples a structured framework in which to have their agreement discussion.

You'll do the work in momentum, identifying your interests, consider your backup plan, and understand the importance of brainstorming ideas to help you reach an agreement. Whether or not you are working through this book alone or with your partner, you'll be in a position to take the reins on the agreement discussion.

In this chapter I will explain how the LEADR-to-yes method works, and how you're going to follow it in your agreement discussion. I'll also give you ideas on managing your partner if they don't play ball.

The LEADR-to-yes approach

I'll start by defining what the LEADR-to-yes stands for:

- *L* stands for *listen*: Listen to what the other speaker is saying. The point of listening is to understand,

not respond, you'll listen with the aim of trying to understand what your partner is saying to you, what they actually mean.
- *E* stands for *express*: You'll take the opportunity to communicate to your partner your interests and why they're important to you. In return, your partner will listen.
- *A* stands for *acknowledge*: You'll acknowledge aloud one another's expressed interests and why they're important to them.
- *D* stands for *discuss*: Together you will select your most preferred brainstormed ideas and begin to workshop them, making improvements as you go to satisfy both of your interests as much as possible, thereby allowing you to reach an agreement.
- *R* stands for *repeat*: You'll guessed it; repeat means you work through this exercise again, unpacking your interests and working them into your preferred brainstormed ideas until you've reached an agreement.

And now I'll cover each of those points in detail:

- *Listen:* Listening involves two steps: the imparting and the receiving of information. Your role in listening is to really *hear* what your partner is saying so you can understand it.

You've probably been in situations where you've spoken to another person and they've not looked you in the eye, or turned away, or had their arms crossed. I'm sure it didn't make you feel as though the person was receptive to what you were saying.

In this listening exercise, you will look your partner in the eye when they're talking to you. Be aware of your body language. Forget crossing your arms or sitting on your hands. Instead, hold your pen and place your hands on top of one another, on the table or on your knees. When your partner finishes speaking, you'll pause for a moment, reflect on what they have said, and write down in dot-point form what you heard and understood your partner to say. The act of writing things down triggers different areas of the brain associated with learning, and this can help with understanding.

- *Express*: This means the imparting of information. For the purpose of this exercise, we'll assume you're sitting next to your partner. When you're expressing to your partner, you'll turn to them and read aloud the notes that you prepared about your interests and why they're important to you. It will be more effective and engaging if you can maintain eye contact and use your notes for reference, rather than reading them word for word. Again, be aware of your body language. Forget crossing your arms or sitting on your hands. Instead, hold your interests paper with one or both hands.

- *Acknowledge*: This means taking the opportunity to clarify or correct any communication misunderstanding that arises. Acknowledging is about ensuring that you and your partner understand what you've said and mean. Remember, you're not setting out to persuade your partner to agree with you, but simply to have them understand what you're saying (Fisher & Ury 2012, p. 38).

When you acknowledge, you'll turn to your partner so that you're facing them. You'll maintain eye contact and refer to your listening notes (the notes you wrote down about what your partner said and their *why*) and say something along the lines of: 'I heard you say … which I understand to mean … is that right? Is there anything you want to add that's important for me to know?'

Your partner may respond by saying something like: 'Yes, that's right' or 'No, that's not quite right, what I meant was …' or 'It's important to me that you know … because …'

- *Discuss:* Once you've identified your interests and their importance to you, communicated them to your partner and there is understanding between you, you'll be in a position to begin the discussion exercise.

  Using the brainstormed ideas, you and your partner will start by circling or highlighting the outcomes that you most prefer. These options will be those that satisfy some of your interests. Depending on the number of brainstormed ideas you've both come up with, you should be able to narrow it down to between three and six.

  Language is important here, because you're not asking one another to agree to outcomes. You'll simply be focusing on the preference (Fisher & Ury 2012, p. 77).

  The next part of the listening exercise will be to unpack each individual outcome that you and your partner have identified, and ask one another questions.

- What do you like about this option?
- What don't you like about this option?
- How do you think it addresses your interests?
- How do you think it addresses my interests?
- What could we do to improve on this option to make it acceptable to you, me or both of us?

You'll see if you can narrow down the preferred outcomes further to one or three only so you're workshopping the ones that have the most potential. Your aim is to think of ways that maximise mutual benefit, improving on the brainstormed outcomes in order to agree.

- *Repeat:* If you and your partner can't agree, you'll repeat. This is not about you both going through the exercises again in exactly the same way you did the first time around. It's more about unpacking to explain how some of the preferred brainstormed outcomes did or did not satisfy your individual needs.

You'll identify whether the disagreement is a data problem. A data problem is where further information is needed to make a firm decision. For example, you might not agree on the value of an asset. Is the disagreement an emotional problem? An emotional problem is where the preferred outcome doesn't address your or your partner's *why* satisfactorily. Try to identify the reason(s) that you don't or can't agree.

If your partner doesn't play ball

Now we'll take a look at a few possible scenarios if your partner is not willing to cooperate.

My partner is delusional: Your partner may say to you, 'If you think I'm walking away for anything less than [*insert unrealistic cash amount*] you're mistaken, and I won't accept anything else.' You know there's no way you have that kind of money. You might be dealing with someone who is disconnected from reality, delusional or out of touch with what's happening. Unfortunately this situation makes communication extremely difficult.

In this case, the LEADR-to-yes method might not be the most effective strategy for bringing you both to a constructive agreement discussion. So what do you do? The first thing to do in this situation is understand that you won't be able to reason with them. Your partner, whether legitimately or not, may feel victimised. They may be in denial and fail to acknowledge wrongdoings on their part that have caused the relationship to end. Their sense of reality may therefore be warped, which means they're unlikely to consider themselves accountable.

How do you manage your partner? How do you redirect their energies and focus back to the problem to be solved? Consider saying, 'I hear what you're saying. Can we talk further about how we solve our problem?'

When it comes to managing their expectations about the financial split, this is where your objective third-party evidence about values and how you present the information becomes crucial. You need to set out the information in a way that is easy to understand; in other words, simple and basic. Consider putting the information in a written summary and giving it to your partner before your agreement discussion or after it.

My partner continues to blame: You can manage your partner by redirecting their focus back to the problem that needs solving by saying, 'I hear what you're saying. Can we talk further about how we solve our problem?' Repeat this as often as needed.

My partner is being positional: This is where you need to assess whether you're able to gain anything by accepting your partner's position instead of deferring to your backup plan. Ask your partner, 'How is your proposal beneficial to meeting my needs and interests as well as your own?' Or ask, 'What are your concerns about the outcomes that I've suggested?'

My partner is into playing games and lying: Trust and transparency are key components of an amicable separation. Understand that if your partner is lying to you or playing games, this is their way of dealing with insecurity and feeling threatened. They are trying to get the upperhand and win. That doesn't mean that you have to be accepting of that behaviour.

When it comes to game playing, acknowledge what appears to be going on and say to your partner, 'I get the feeling that you're trying to confuse me' or 'These concepts are confusing to me, let's take it back a bit and talk it through in smaller parts.'

If your partner is blatantly and repeatedly lying to you, you'll need to assess whether it's worth continuing the agreement discussion, or whether you need to engage a professional to help you.

We don't seem to be getting anywhere: If you're in this situation, there are a few possible reasons. You and your partner may not be following LEADR-to-yes properly, you could just be tired, or you need a third person to help you both get perspective and lead the agreement discussion.

Chapter 9
Endorse Your Agreement

Throughout this book, I've referred to making your separation agreements 'official'. When I say official, I simply mean getting your agreement recognised legally under the appropriate legislation. The advantages to endorsing your agreement by making it official might include:

- Emotional benefits: Relief, joy, happiness or peace of mind knowing you can move forward.

- Psychological benefits: Feelings of stability and security about the future, whether it's about the split of finances, or your children's care arrangements and financial support for them.
- Financial benefits: These include the ability to begin planning and rebuilding yourself financially, and protecting your future wealth: future inheritances, lotto wins, superannuation and the like.

    You could save on the cost of stamp duty for the transfer of real estate, cars or shares in certain states and territories. If you are transferring your share in real estate to your partner due to 'the breakdown of the relationship', then you may be entitled to a stamp-duty reduction, or exemption on the purchase of a new property.
- Stability: This includes a set routine for your children regarding their care arrangements.
- Security: Knowing the minimum amount of time that you have with your children.
- Understanding: Knowledge shared by you and your partner about your children's care arrangements and matters relating to them.
- Enforcement: The ability to legally enforce your agreement.
- Clear expectations: Understanding of the obligations to do or not do certain things; minimising future

disagreements, confusion, misinterpretation or misunderstanding.

Get ready, because you're about to put some divorce lawyers out of business and save yourself a small fortune. I've broken this chapter into three sections:

- Parenting agreements: the different ways this can be endorsed and what's involved in making the agreement official
- Financial agreements: the different ways this can be endorsed and what's involved in making the agreement official
- Divorce, maintenance and child support: an explanation of all need-to-know information

Parenting Agreements

When it comes to endorsing your parenting agreement, you have two options:

- Parenting plan
- Parenting consent order

In this section I will cover the differences between these two options and explain what parenting agreements typically cover. I'll explain the paperwork to be prepared for each option and give you some examples where parents opted to endorse their parenting agreement in one of these two ways for different reasons.

What is a parenting agreement?

A *parenting agreement* does not have to be official. You and your partner can choose to leave it as an informal verbal or written agreement, for example in an email, or you can make it a formal legal agreement. (I've outlined at the beginning of this chapter some of the benefits of making your parenting agreement legal.) The question of whether you should make it legal or keep it informal comes down to the advice your lawyer gives you, if you opt to get legal advice.

A parenting agreement can deal with any of the following matters:

- Who your children live with
- Who your children spend time with, and how often, and whether the arrangements are to change over time as the children grow older

CHAPTER 9: ENDORSE YOUR AGREEMENT

- How long-term decisions about the children are made (known as parental responsibility)
- What happens on special occasions such as birthdays, Mother's Day, Father's Day, Christmas, Easter, half-sibling birthdays
- What happens during the school term and school holidays
- Phone contact between the children and each parent
- Financial support for the children
- How parenting disputes are to be resolved
- Where handover is to happen, and how
- Which daycare, schools and medical centres your children go to
- Restraints on parents taking illegal substances or consuming excessive alcohol
- Interstate and overseas travel
- How you and your partner will communicate with one another about the children
- How you and your partner will exchange information about your children's schooling and medical matters
- Anything to do with your child's 'care, welfare and development'
- The possibility of either parent relocating with the children
- The children's surnames

- What's to happen if either of you die before your children turn eighteen
- Review date for the care arrangements
- Requirement that you go to mediation in the future

What is a parenting plan?

A *parenting plan* is a written agreement between a child's parents that deals with at least one of the things in the above list. Both parents sign and date the document. A parenting plan has to be made 'free from any threat, duress or coercion', and does not need to be registered with the court or anyone else.

It's important to note that a parenting plan is not legally binding or enforceable. If you want to have a legally binding parenting agreement, you need a parenting consent order (see below). If you or your partner can't agree about parenting arrangements and ask the court to make a decision, the judge will take into account what any recent parenting plan says if doing so would be in your children's best interests.

CHAPTER 9: ENDORSE YOUR AGREEMENT

What is a parenting consent order?

A *parenting consent order* is agreed to by a child's parents and is signed off on (approved) by the court. Some important things to know about a parenting consent order:

- The order applies to each child named in the parenting order until they turn eighteen, marry or enter into a de facto relationship.
- The order is binding and enforceable by the court; there can be consequences if it is not followed.
- The order is made only when the court is satisfied that the proposed care arrangements for the children are in their best interests.
- The court will not follow up with the parents to check that they're abiding by the order.
- Typically, the police don't have the power to intervene and force the parents to comply; only the court can enforce parenting consent orders or parenting orders.
- Neither parent can take the children out of Australia without a court order or the non-travelling parent's written permission, and to do so would be a criminal offence.
- Depending on what the parenting consent order specifically says, the parents may not be allowed

to hinder, interfere or prevent one another's compliance with the order, for example, by refusing to return the children, not allowing communication between the children and the other parent, or hindering parental responsibility being carried out.
- Depending on what the parenting consent order stipulates, the parents may be obliged to do certain things. For example, if an order stipulates equal shared parental responsibility, both parents must consult with one another and make a genuine effort to reach an agreement about any major long-term decision that may affect the children. Both parents are obliged to encourage the children to have a meaningful relationship with the other parent.

Failure to follow a parenting consent order

Things happen in life. Kids refuse to go to the other parent's house, one of the kids has a sleepover on the weekend when they're scheduled to be at Mum's, or there's a soccer presentation scheduled on Wednesday night when the kids are supposed to call Dad.

It's therefore up to you and your partner to make a reasonable attempt to comply with the parenting consent order. This means working together to come up with alternative solutions.

If you or your partner intentionally fail to comply with an order, make no reasonable attempt to comply, intentionally prevent compliance or aid and abet a breach, then a judge could find that you or your partner breached a parenting consent order.

The parent wanting to enforce the parenting consent order has to submit an application to the court asking them to deal with the non-compliance. There are consequences for not following a parenting consent order. The court can:

- order that the non-compliant parent attend a post-separation parenting program, or facilitate time between the children and the parent who missed out on time as a result of the contravention
- decide to vary, discharge, suspend or revive an earlier parenting order
- order that the non-compliant parent be issued with a fine
- order that the non-compliant parent reimburse or give financial compensation to the parent who has suffered financially as a result of the contravention
- order that the non-compliant parent go to gaol.

Choosing a parenting plan or parenting consent order

Which one is right for you and your partner, a parenting plan, or a parenting consent order? That depends on several factors:

- Do you believe that the proposed arrangements are in your children's best interests, including whether it is appropriate for their age and consistent with their developmental needs?
- Is there a review date? Is the agreement intended to cover the children's care arrangements from now until they're eighteen, or do you want to agree on what's to happen for the next two years, then five years and so?
- Do you think your partner will abide by the agreement?
- Is there a risk of your partner changing their mind about the agreement or refusing to give or return the children to you? Do you want to secure a minimum amount of time with your kids, or cement the current arrangements?

Importantly, your decision as to which to choose also depends on the legal advice you receive, if any. It might be in your children's best interests to have something that is a bit less binding so you can tweak it here and there, particularly if you've got young children.

Here is an example of a possible scenario.

Sam and Stevie separated six months ago. They have two kids together, Kate, who is eighteen months, and Orla, who is three years. They've agreed that given Kate and Orla's young age, it's in the children's best interests that they initially live primarily with Sam, and spend regular time with Stevie.

They decide to make their *parenting agreement* official in the form of a *parenting plan* because they intend to update it in the future. They agree that the parenting plan will allow them the flexibility to make changes as often as needed to accommodate the children's needs as they grow older.

Here is a second example.

Sarah and James have separated. They have three kids together. They've agreed that the kids will live with James nine nights per fortnight and five nights per fortnight with Sarah. Each parent will have the kids for half of the school holidays and share special occasions.

Sarah is concerned that James will later reduce her time with the kids so she wants to have certainty about their current agreement. They agree to make their *parenting agreement* official in the form of a *parenting consent order* because that arrangement, unless they agree otherwise, will be in place until the kids turn eighteen (assuming the children don't marry or enter into a de-facto relationship before then).

Endorsing your parenting agreement

Once you've reached an agreement, make a dot point summary about it. Work out whether you want to make it official in a parenting consent order or parenting plan. Then decide whether you want to prepare your agreement paperwork or get a lawyer to do it all for you.

With the availability of online information and resources, if you have the time I'd encourage you to have a go at preparing your own draft parenting agreement. Check out 'Parenting Orders: What You Need to Know Handbook' at the Attorney-General's Department for examples of wording

CHAPTER 9: ENDORSE YOUR AGREEMENT

that lawyers tend to use for parenting agreements both in parenting consent orders and parenting plans.

With a parenting consent order, there are two documents that need to be prepared:

- Application for (parenting) consent order: This is a pretty long court form that asks for basic information such as your name, date of birth, contact information, relationship details and information about your kids and their proposed care arrangements. Although it is long, the questions are fairly basic and easy to answer.
- Proposed parenting consent order: This is the legalese document, which specifically says what's to happen when it comes to the kids, including who they live with and spend time with, parental responsibility and the like. This does have to be correctly formatted in the court's form of order.

For a parenting plan, there is just the one document that needs to be prepared. You can get the wording from the Attorney General's Department handbook and title your document 'Parenting Plan'.

Finally, consider getting some legal advice about your parenting agreement that covers the meaning and effect of it, and your obligations. Once the paperwork is prepared and finalised, review, sign and date it.

For a parenting consent order, you'll need to take the extra step of submitting the signed paperwork to the court to be reviewed and signed off on.

> You can prepare your own draft Parenting Plan with the appropriate wording and clauses all online, by simply answering some questions about your parenting agreement. Visit separatetogether.com.au/online-store/ to find our more.

Financial agreements

When it comes to endorsing your financial agreement, you have two options:

- Binding financial agreement
- Financial consent order

I will cover the differences between these two options and explain the paperwork to be prepared for each option.

CHAPTER 9: ENDORSE YOUR AGREEMENT

Financial separation agreement options

- *Binding financial agreement (BFA):* This is a private agreement that sets out who is to keep what, how the agreement is to be carried out, and when. Because the court doesn't sign off on the agreement, you and your partner have to get independent legal advice from separate lawyers about the agreement and its effect on your rights, and the advantages and disadvantages of entering into the agreement.

   The legislation on BFAs is fairly prescriptive and has to be strictly adhered to in order to make it a valid, binding agreement. You really do have to use lawyers to get your financial separation agreement made official this way.

- *Financial consent order (FCO):* This type of agreement is signed off by the Family Court. Essentially, paperwork gets prepared setting out who keeps what, how the agreement is to be carried out and when, and this is then submitted to the court to be reviewed and signed off on. Typically, the couple doesn't have to go to court.

What happens if the financial separation is not endorsed?

Aside from the benefits listed at the beginning of this chapter, you won't be able to do a superannuation split if you don't endorse your financial separation agreement in one of the two ways described. Your financial ties may not be severed, which importantly means that you and your partner can make claims against one another in the future.

Divorced couples have twelve months from the date of the divorce to reach a financial separation agreement and endorse it or apply to the court for a decision about a financial split. De-facto couples have two years from the date of separation to reach a financial separation agreement and endorse it, or apply to the court for a decision. Anything that you and your partner receive, earn or incur could therefore be up for grabs—available to be split between you.

Financial consent order or binding financial agreement?

Which option is right for you, a financial consent order (FCO) or a binding financial agreement (BFA)? There are several reasons why lawyers sometimes recommend that their clients make their financial separation agreement official in a BFA:

- The agreement is outside of what the law says is fair and therefore the court is unlikely to sign off on the agreement reached.
- The agreement might be extremely complex due to substantial wealth and a complex asset pool.
- You might want the agreement to remain strictly confidential.
- The lawyer may have simply been taught that BFAs are the better way to go over FCOs.

If you're unsure about which option is best for you and your partner, ask an experienced family lawyer for their advice based on your circumstances.

My firm, Separate Together, specialises in preparing the legal paperwork to make a financial separation agreement official in a financial consent orders (FCO). Through experience, I've discovered this to be a simpler, more cost- and time-efficient way of facilitating the outcome my clients want.

Making the financial separation agreement official

There are three steps to follow in making your financial separation agreement official in a FCO:

Step 1: Put together a dot-point summary of your agreement.

Step 2: Prepare the agreement paperwork, which will consist of two documents:

- Application for (financial) consent order: This is a court form that I refer to as the numbers document. In addition to setting out contact details and dates of birth for you and your partner, plus information about any children you have, you have to list your assets, debts and superannuation, and their values. This form asks questions designed to draw out the relevant information for the court to decide whether the proposed agreement is within the range of what the law says is fair.
- Proposed order by consent: I call this the nuts-and-bolts document as it spells out what's to happen as part of your agreement: who keeps what, how the agreement will be carried out and when. There

is some technical legal jargon that needs to be included to deal with any complicated issues and comply with the court's requirements.

If you're prepared to do more of the work yourself to minimise fees and lawyer involvement, you can download the application for consent order from the Family Court website: http://www.familycourt.gov.au/wps/wcm/connect/fcoaweb/forms-and-fees/court-forms/diy-kits/kit-diy-application-consent-orders.

Alternatively, you can complete it online by registering with the Commonwealth Court's portal: https://www.comcourts.gov.au/pip/individual/new.

To minimise fees and reduce the amount of time it takes to get the paperwork prepared, you could give the lawyer a dot-point summary of your agreement, a written explanation of how you came to your agreement, or the list that you prepared of your and your partner's separate and joint assets, debts and superannuation, and the values.

What you want the lawyer to do is fairly simple and is easily scoped. Ask them for an obligation-free fixed price to prepare your agreement paperwork. You can then shop around and see how this compares to other law firms and decide who you want to go with.

Step 3: Before signing and submitting to the court, consider getting advice from a lawyer about your agreement as well as your agreement paperwork. I strongly encourage this. The advice from the lawyer should include:

- Notice of whether the proposed agreement is an appropriate outcome according to what the law says
- Advice about the relevance of parenting, divorce and child support support and maintenance
- Advice about the effect of your agreement on your rights, entitlements and obligations under the *Family Law Act 1975*
- Advice on the drafting of the agreement paperwork
- Steps you need to take in order to implement the agreement

When the paperwork is prepared and finalised, review and sign it.

Step 4: Submit the signed paperwork to the court for the court to review and sign off on. Once the court signs off on your financial consent order, you'll need to carry out what the agreement says. This could mean selling the house; transferring the house, shares or cars; divvying up the furniture; or arranging for the superannuation split.

The court won't check to see if you've followed the agreement. If someone hasn't abided by the agreement the person wanting compliance has to ask the court to intervene to enforce it.

Divorce, maintenance and child support

In chapter 6, I covered what the law says about child support, explaining your legal obligations to provide for your kids financially after separation. In this section I will explain the different ways you can endorse your child-support agreement (if different to assessed child support) and give you some things to think about when it comes to the practicalities of the agreement.

Child-support agreement

If you and your partner agree to contribute financially towards your kids' expenses above what the child-support agency (Department of Human Services) may calculate to be your legal obligations, you can make that financial-support agreement official and binding in one of two ways: a limited child support agreement (LSA), or a binding child support agreement (BCSA).

Perhaps the most significant differences between a LSA and a BCSA are:

- A LSA lasts for three years only; a BCSA lasts until a child is eighteen years (although this can be extended)
- Independent legal advice is not required for a LSA; independent legal advice is required for a BCSA

There are a few important things to consider with regard to both LSAs and BCSAs:

- Your agreement should be registered with the child-support agency so it can be enforced.
- Before you sign your final LSA or BCSA, your draft agreement should be approved by the child-support agency.
- Get specific advice from a family lawyer about the enforceability of what your agreement says about non-periodic child-support expenses. These are those irregular expenses that crop up from time to time, for example, extracurricular activities, and medical and school expenses.
- Consider including clauses in your agreement that stipulate what's to happen regarding your respective financial obligations for the children if either you

or your partner become ill, unemployed, suffer an injury, die, or either income increases above or drops below a certain amount.

- Have a think about including clauses that cover how you and your partner are going to pay your kids' expenses. When considering this, also think about the degree of interaction you're prepared to have with one another going forward and whether there is trust between you. Here are a few ideas:
    - Have a joint bank account where one or both of you contributes funds, and each person has a card that is used to pay for your kids' expenses.
    - Reimburse the parent who may have paid for the children's expenses upfront.
    - Get third parties to issue you and your partner separate invoices for their fees in the agreed portions. Sometimes third parties may not do this as both parents can be considered jointly severally liable, or the parent who registered the child for the activity is the one who is one hundred percent liable.
    - Agree that parent A will pay to parent B a specified amount each week or month that is intended to cover all non-periodic and/or periodic expenses in relation to your child for the year. It is up to parent B to direct that payment towards the child's various expenses.

It might be that you do one or a combination of the above ideas for different expenses, but it is important that you and your partner are both clear on how you're actually going to carry out the agreement. There are benefits, risks, advantages and disadvantages to the above ideas that a lawyer is best placed to speak with you further about.

Maintenance agreements

As I covered in chapter 1, maintenance may be relevant where a person has a reasonable need, they can't pay for their reasonable need themselves from their income and the other person has a capacity to pay—a buffer between their income and expenditure.

In this section I will explain briefly what your maintenance agreement could cover (if it's relevant to you) and the reasons why you want to endorse a maintenance agreement.

If maintenance is relevant, you and your partner have several options. One of you could make an ongoing payment to the other for a period of time, or until a specific event happens; one of you could pay expenses on the other person's behalf; one of you could receive more of the assets now as part of your financial split as lump-sum maintenance instead of an ongoing payment arrangement; or neither of you pay maintenance to the other person.

You can have this agreement drawn up in a binding financial agreement (maintenance BFA). You will both need to get independent legal advice in order to have your agreement made official in a maintenance BFA. Maintenance is separate from child support, and normally it is also separate from your financial separation agreement.

There are three reasons for doing a maintenance BFA: 1) you and your partner have agreed to lump-sum maintenance and you want it to be enforceable, 2) you and your partner have agreed that one of you will pay maintenance to the other for an agreed amount for a specified period of time or until a specific event happens, or 3) a maintenance BFA will prevent your partner making a claim against you for maintenance in the future and vice versa.

Divorce

As I covered in chapter 1, to apply for divorce you have to be separated for more than twelve months. You can be separated and living under the same roof.

In this section I will give a brief explanation of the major differences between applying for divorce by yourself or applying jointly with your partner.

Typically, applying for divorce by yourself is more expensive. This is because you have to arrange what's called service of your divorce application on your spouse, which may mean that you have to use a professional process server to give the paperwork to your spouse. There is also some additional paperwork that has to be prepared and submitted to the court, which means additional legal fees (if you use a lawyer) and the process server's fee.

If you apply for divorce by yourself and you or your spouse have a child under the age of eighteen years, whether together or from a previous relationship, you have to go to the court on the divorce hearing date to satisfy the court that there are appropriate care arrangements in place for the child. If you apply for divorce jointly, then typically neither of you will need to go to the court for the divorce hearing to satisfy the court about any childcare arrangements. The court can determine your application on the paperwork you've submitted instead.

Divorce applications can be submitted online.

I suggest that you update your estate plan. This includes your will, enduring power of attorney, and superannuation death-beneficiary nomination.

Chapter 10
Putting It All into Practice

You're almost there. You're almost ready to get started. By now, you have learned how your life could change when or if the decision to separate is made. You know your options when it comes to either working on your relationship or making the decision to separate.

You have knowledge about what the law says in general terms about the split of the pie, parenting, child support, maintenance and divorce after separation, and you know the things to do in order to progress your separation to reach an agreement with your partner. You know how important it is to have a backup plan, and how to go about developing one.

You're aware of the different processes available to you to reach a separation agreement with your partner, which don't involve going to court.

You're aware of how advice from professionals can help you plan for your future and you can identify your interests in order to think big picture and focus on reaching a final agreement. You have the tools to help facilitate a productive agreement discussion with your partner.

Before putting it all into practice, there are a few more practical aspects to think about in preparation for your agreement discussion. I'll cover these and give you an action plan if you and your partner are unable to reach a final agreement. Then, you'll be ready to get started.

Venue and time

It might seem obvious, but have you and your partner thought about where you're going to meet and when? Meeting in a public place could reduce the risk of tension or emotions escalating, but consider whether you feel comfortable talking about your private issues in public.

CHAPTER 10: PUTTING IT ALL INTO PRACTICE

Meeting at one of your homes could give you some privacy, and leaves the option open for leaving the house if things become uncomfortable for either of you.

When deciding on a meeting place, think about who's going to be around—kids, housemates or family—and whether the territory is neutral enough for you both. Consider the time of day that you meet. Will your agreement discussion be productive if you meet at the end of the day after work, or after night shift? Are you able to take leave from work, start early, or start late in order to have your agreement discussion? Ideally, for your agreement discussion to be productive you both want to feel energised, engaged, comfortable and as safe as possible.

Duration: How long will the agreement discussion go for? Agreeing on a time limit for the discussion sets boundaries and helps in managing one another's expectations. Neither of you have to be that person who ends the conversation.

Start by allocating an hour and a half to have the agreement discussion. It's usually by the second hour that people need a small break. You can always continue the discussion beyond the initial agreed amount of time, but keep it flexible by saying, for example, 'Let's talk for an extra thirty minutes and see how we go.' You want to have a productive discussion about reaching an agreement and be meaningfully engaged. You don't want to be wearing one another down.

Preparation: Assuming that you've worked out the date, time and how long the agreement discussion will last, now it's time to power your brain by taking the following steps. You don't want to get h-angry, so feed yourself a proper meal before you meet. Make sure you have a good night's sleep the night before. Get organised by pulling your financial documents together, updating the financial list, and going over your list of interests and your backup plan. Familiarise yourself with the meeting exercise, and be prepared. Put out water, pens and paper so you can both take notes. Be sure to have two copies of our suggested meeting exercise.

What to do if you can't agree

If you appear to be reaching a stalemate, take a five- or ten-minute breather. Then regroup and ask one another, 'How do you think we went?' or 'How are you feeling?' Talk about it. Complete the last meeting-exercise item, which is the where-to-from-here action plan.

Ask the following questions: Do either of you need further information in order to progress? If yes, what information is needed? Do you need to get a third person to help you? If yes, who should that person be?

Consider rescheduling another time to get together and pick up where you left off. Schedule the next catch-up within a fortnight so you don't lose momentum and motivation. The longer things drag on for, the more uncertainty there can be. Uncertainty can breed insecurity, which could leave one or both of you feeling threatened.

Two's company, three can be a good crowd

Yes, you read correctly—three can be a good crowd.

A third person could help you and your partner in your agreement discussion, whether you decide to involve them from the get-go, or after you try to reach an agreement first between yourselves.

In considering who that third person should be, you can involve a trusted mutual friend, family member, or third-party mediator or organisation. The benefit to you is that if you've followed the steps outlined in this book—acceptance, momentum, interests, consideration of a backup plan, advice, brainstorming, and following the LEADR-to-yes method—you've done the foundational work that professional third-party mediators would ordinarily take you through.

Basically, if you have a go at trying to have the agreement discussion between yourselves and it isn't as productive as you'd hoped, seriously consider involving a trusted third person.

When you've agreed

Once you've reached an agreement, you'll need to prepare a dot-point summary. Review the chapter on endorsing your agreement, which covers the different ways you can make your separation agreement official, the paperwork that's involved, and the ways to go about getting it prepared.

Getting started

Well, it now seems that you're at the pointy end of the book and you'll be ready to get started.

Before you meet I'd suggest going over one last time chapters 4, 5, 6 and 7. Also, familiarise yourself with the meeting exercises that follow. At first glance, some of the exercises may read as being wishy-washy but there is a point to doing them, which is to focus your energies and efforts on the problem you're trying to solve together, whilst acknowledging that you're both human and have feelings.

Best of luck!

Our Agreement Discussion—Meeting Exercises
Date of agreement talk

Venue	
Start time	
Agreed finish time	
We will talk about:	
Checklist	☑ We both have our financial documents with us ☑ We have the appraisals and valuations (as applicable) ☑ We both have a list of our interests ☑ At least one of us has a copy of this meeting exercise/the handbook ☑ We have a copy of our own backup plans ☑ We have updated the asset list ☑ We have pens and paper ☑ We have a whiteboard/butcher's paper

Exercise 1: Housekeeping (five minutes)

Opening: In alphabetical order using first names, you will read aloud the opening:

- We're here to work together to reach an agreement about final matters following our separation.
- We're committed to working through this together so we can move forward in a positive way.
- We're open to all possibilities and ideas that we come up with.

Rules of engagement: The other person will read aloud the rules of engagement (ask each other if you want to add any more ground rules, and if so add them to the list):

- We will remove blame from the discussion and instead will attack the problem together.
- We will show one another respect. We will listen and engage meaningfully with what the other person is saying. We will not interrupt one another.
- We will not use threats of court or intimidation.
- We acknowledge that we could both be worse off and that it's in both our interests, emotionally and

financially, for us to work together as a team to reach a final agreement.

The elephant: Addressing the elephant in the room, both of you will pick two words each from the list that mostly accurately describe how you're feeling right now:

- Worried
- Optimistic
- Excited
- Nervous
- Anxious
- Frustrated
- Angry
- Sad
- Upset
- Doubtful
- Hopeful

Exercise 2: Brainstorming (ten minutes)

Having read Chapter 7 of *Splitting Up Together*, you're now going to brainstorm all of the potential agreement outcomes available. Remember, you're not judging whether they're good or bad ideas, or if you like them or not.

Exercise 3: LEADR to yes

Familiarise yourself with Chapter 8 of *Splitting Up Together*.

Listen (seven minutes each): In alphabetical order using first names, you will listen and write notes in the boxes below.

Express (seven minutes each): Take turns in expressing to one another your interests (obviously the person who isn't listening will be expressing). The person who is expressing their interests will say something like: 'It's important to me that ... and this is because ...' or 'I'm concerned about ... and this is because ...'

Interests	Because

Acknowledge (six minutes each): You: 'When you said XYZ, I understood you to mean …' Partner: 'Yes, that's right' or 'No, what I meant was … Does that make sense?'

Discuss (thirty minutes): Pick a total of four to six options that you both prefer and believe have the potential to satisfy both of your interests. How can you improve each option so that it satisfies both of you?

Repeat (twenty minutes): The repeat exercise is not about you going through exactly the same things as you did the first time around. It's more about unpacking to explain how some of the brainstormed options that you and your partner mostly favoured did or did not meet your needs.

Exercise 4: Wrap up (ten minutes)

Thank one another. Ask, 'How are you feeling?'

Closing:	☐ Thank one another
	☐ Discuss the where to from here

Comments/action plan:

Download Your Free Kick-Starter Separation Pack

Separated and don't know what to do next?

The free *Kick-Starter Separation Pack* is designed to pull all of the relevant information that you and your partner need in order to work out what's available to be split financially between the two of you. Use it to get legal advice, or not. For the free download, go to:
separatetogether.com.au/online-store

Connect with Siobhan Mullins at:

Website:
separatetogether.com.au
Facebook:
facebook.com/SeparateTogether/

About the Author

Siobhan is a collaboratively trained divorce lawyer. She is the founder of Separate Together, Australia's leading online family-law firm, which specialises in preparing the paperwork to make separation agreements official, integrating technology to offer a unique service menu at affordable fixed prices, reducing lawyer involvement.

Siobhan's approach to the practice of law has seen her and her firm listed as a finalist for various industry and business awards. Siobhan is based in Canberra and works with separating individuals and couples from across Australia and overseas, helping people to separate, but together.

Siobhan is a contributor to a range of mainstream and online media. You can keep in touch with Siobhan on LinkedIn or by subscribing to her blog (https://separatetogether.com.au).

Bibliography

Australian Bureau of Statistics 2016, *Marriages and divorces, Australia 2016* Cat. no. 3310.0, Australian Bureau of Statistics, Canberra, accessed 28 October 2018 <http://www.abs.gov.au/ausstats/abs@.nsf/mf/3310.0>

Australian Psychology Society 2015, *Stress and wellbeing: How Australians are coping with life*, accessed 28 October 2018 < https://www.headsup.org.au/docs/default-source/default-document-library/stress-and-wellbeing-in-australia-report.pdf?sfvrsn=7f08274d_4>

Caruana, C., Ferro, A., Smyth, B., Weston, R., Whitfield, C., Wolcott, R. & Qu, L 2004, *Parent-child contact and post separation parenting arrangements*, Research Report No. 9 Australian Institute of Family Studies, Melbourne

Family Court of Australia 2018, *Annual Report 2017–2018,* Canberra

Family Law Act 1975 (Cth)

Federal Circuit Court of Australia 2018, *Annual Report 2017–2018*, Canberra

Fisher, R. & Ury, W 2012, *Getting to yes: negotiating an agreement without giving in,* 3rd edn, Random House Business Books, London

Hewitt, B 2008, *Marriage breakdown in Australia: social correlates, gender and initiator status*, no. 35, Department of Families, Housing, Community Services & Indigenous Affairs, Canberra

Relationships Australia 2011, *Issues and concerns for Australian relationships today,* Canberra, accessed 28 October 2018 < https://www.relationships.org.au/what-we-do/research/australian-relationships-indicators/relationships-indicator-2011>

www.ingramcontent.com/pod-product-compliance
Lightning Source LLC
Chambersburg PA
CBHW070059020526
44112CB00034B/1868